You Don't Know *Jack* About Strategic Planning

By Jack Rahaim

I0474985

"He Who Fails To Plan, Plans To Fail"
Winston Churchill
"What The Hell Just Happened"?
Anonymous CEO Who Didn't Plan

This is **not** your father's book on Strategy. This is a no-holds-barred look at real organizations, real planning processes, written with deliberately little *consultant-speak* and it can guide you and your organization to sustainable success.

Based on the learnings from 20 years of working with some of the best and brightest minds in organizations in the U.S., Europe and Japan, this book will teach you how to think *Strategically* and how to turn that thinking into a defensible competitive advantage.

Jack's edgy style, use of examples from many industries and time-tested worksheet exercises will keep you reading and learning.

Jack also teaches you how to create a *Strategic Plan* for *your* organization and how to plan a successful implementation.

Jack's other best-selling book *No More Meetings From Hell* has been used by organizations throughout the world as *the bible* of meeting and process design.

You Don't Know *Jack* About Strategic Planning

by Jack Rahaim

Copyright © 2011 by Jack Rahaim

Dedication

I'll separate my dedications into three categories: professional, personal connections and personal.

Professional Inspiration The pioneers who led the way for the rest of us: Bruce Henderson of the Boston Consulting Group; Michael Porter of the Harvard Business School; Regis McKenna of Regis McKenna, Inc. (crafter of Apple's early strategies); Michael Hammer who introduced the world to Business Process Redesign and Russell Ackoff of the Wharton School who taught the world about Systems Thinking. I stand on your shoulders and am appreciative of what I've learned from you.

Personal Connections These are the folks with whom I've worked over the years and from whom I've learned about thinking *strategically*: Ilan Meshoulam, the first manager who 'got' me and encouraged what he saw, Jeff Singer and Ray Locke, formerly of Digital Equipment Corporation's HR Systems Group, from whom I learned the concept of having users *pull* on a solution; Dennis O'Connor, who was a visionary in the field of emerging technologies and taught me how to generate excitement for ideas still in formation; Bob Clark, my first manager at DEC who encouraged me to learn about the culture before trying to get anything accomplished and for his understanding of, and sense of humor about, organizational dynamics; Gerhard Friedrich, who taught me how to structure complex concepts for senior managers; Frank Lynch, who taught me to build on other people's dreams; Tim Parris who taught me that a Strategic Plan can be drawn on a napkin over a cup of coffee before heading out for a day's sail; Gary Brock, who taught me to think about cause and effect many levels deeper than I knew even existed; Gerald Bryant, from whom I learned how to conduct an appropriately structured strategic planning process.

Personal Support

I especially dedicate this book to my two sons, Jason and Matt, two of the best men I know and who teach me something new every time we speak; my grandson, Aiden, who brings such joy to our lives and has taught me everything I know about NASCAR. In addition, the support of former clients and now close friends like Deb Nikkel and John Mancuso has given me the faith that what I have to say in this book is important and encouraged my lifestyle of living on a boat *and* in New York.

My life has been shaped by many close friendships, especially those of Mal Welch, who taught me how to laugh at *the man*, Phil Sardella, who taught me to think non-linearly, Edd Kalehoff, who taught me that you can make a really good living doing what you love, Donna Parrish, for her love and support and Peter Sass, who taught me to be myself at work.

TABLE OF CONTENTS

Introduction

I've spent over 20 years advising some of the best and brightest managers in the world on how to craft strategies for their organizations. During this time, I've come to this conclusion: *most* senior managers do not have any *real* understanding of *what* strategies are or *how* to create them for their organization. You see, most managers have never been taught to *think* strategically. It doesn't mean that they're not smart enough to do this; often they'll marvel at a company like Apple, Google or even Ford (in the past few years) and talk eloquently about how these companies have created strategies that have made them successful. What they can't do, however, is understand the thought processes that lead to coherent, successful strategies.

Ask them to create *strategies* for *their own* organizations, however, and they will stare at a blank piece of paper for days and, then, out of desperation, they'll create a document which is comprised mostly of academic/consulting models which don't quite fit, platitudes such as *to be the best....to provide value add....etc.*) and a disconnected list of tactics, goals and objectives. In addition, these *Strategic Plans* usually lack a coherent roadmap for how the tactics, goals and objectives will be achieved.

To complete the plan, they'll add in a bit of *French Pastry* by mixing in the latest buzz phrases such as: *move the needle, value proposition, customer-facing, e-anything, etc.*, slap a cover on the sucker and send it out to a selective list of skeptical senior managers...believing that they now have a *strategic plan!* They then stage a ½ day meeting once a year to discuss the plan and then get on with their lives.

The other dynamic that explains why senior managers don't take strategic planning seriously is that, in many organizations, it's an exercise in futility. You see, many organizations are run by just a handful of managers who sit in an 'inner circle'; of these, perhaps only two or three people make all of the really big decisions and it's left to everyone else to implement them.   Is it any wonder that most managers treat the Strategic Planning Process as a game and simply go through the motions, traffic in the use of the *consultant-speak* buzz lexicon of the day, and then go back to managing their departments?

Note: If you're unclear about the terms *Mission, Vision, Strategy, etc.,* take a peak at the **Definition of Terms** later in the book.

Why This Matters I'll talk later about the strategic errors that caused the failure and collapse of a company that I worked at for 14 years. That experience has shaped my thinking *and feelings* about organizations and their success or failure. You see, 120,000 employees were impacted by the failure to plan strategically. In addition, thousands more working for suppliers, distributors and customers were significantly affected by the failure to get the future right. Even though, by then, I had left the company to start my own consulting business, Strategic Planning, or the failure to do it right, got very personal the day this company closed its doors.

The Purpose Of This Book

I've captured the lessons learned in observing, guiding and, in some cases reluctantly driving organizations as they created Strategic Plans. It's clear to me that a major stumbling block for organizations is that they don't know what a Strategic Plan is or how to create one. In this book, I will work with you to develop an understanding of Strategy and show you how to create a Strategic Plan. This doesn't mean that you'll become a Jedi Knight of Strategic Planning simply by reading this book, any more than you'd become a Jimmie Johnson-like driver by examining a map of the Daytona Speedway; you'd simply know what the track looks like, where the turns are, where the pit stops are, etc. As important as this information is, it alone doesn't suddenly make you a successful NASCAR driver.

Speaking of racing, one of the best descriptions of the challenges facing today's managers was in the form of an analogy that I heard on NPR with the champion racer, Mario Andretti.

When asked to talk about what makes auto racing so challenging, he gave a masters class in management. Essentially he said that you are moving at hellacious speeds with another vehicle just inches off your fender...you've got to be *totally* focused on the *now*. At the same time, you know you have a turn coming up, everything is about to change and you've got to be ready for that...i.e., in addition to the now, you've got to be totally focused on the near future. And, as if that wasn't difficult enough, you have a strategy for the race...and you need to be *totally* focused on that. Sound like your day?

Reading this book will give you some powerful ways to think about strategy and guide you through the process. It will hopefully keep you from driving your organization into a ditch or, just as sadly, running out of gas.

The hard part of Strategic Planning has always been, and always will be, the critical thinking that enables organizations to craft a sustainable competitive advantage. I hope to help you sharpen those thinking skills through explaining the process and showing you how other organizations have created successful (and some, not so successful) strategies, as well as through putting you through a number of exercises and some coaching.

The Dirty Little Secret of Strategic Planning Processes Today

Ask most senior managers whether there is a *meaningful* Strategic Planning process in place in their organization and they'll most-likely respond in one of two ways:

- They'll roll their eyes and indicate that there is a very cumbersome process, driven by highly paid Staff which, upon its completion, no one pays much attention to; they'll also say that there's no relationship between what the plan espouses as being important and the ways budgets are allocated. What's interesting about this lack of strategic *thinking* is that the same players, when discussing strategies of *other* organizations seem to both *get* and value the thinking that went into the planning of those other organizations and/or are quick to criticize other organizations for not having viable strategies....or....

- They'll rave about how powerful the plan is, how open and inclusive the process has been and, then, after some probing, you'll find out that they are the same folks who created and drive the planning *process*, not the managers who *should have* had input into the plan and who have to implement it.

The sad truth is that most organizations do what looks very much *like* Strategic Planning: front end data gathering, analysis and, at the back end of the process, a deck of PowerPoint slides with intricate, beautifully colored diagrams.

After reading a number of these plans, one walks away struck by the lack of any *real* strategic thinking or creativity. Let me be clear, there are some very bright people involved in strategic planning; it's just that the process itself is broken, has become formulaic and is almost entirely void of the kind of thinking we'd expect of a exercise that has the word *Strategic* attached to it.

It's also true that, in many cases, the folks who create the plans have never spent time in the field with customers and sales people and have not been taught to think and plan strategically. As you read about once-dominant companies who are no longer serious players in their industries, perhaps you'll begin asking the hard questions about the content of *your* plan and aspire to something greater.

In addition, I've always thought that publications such as the Harvard Business Review have played an important role in the development of strategic thinking and, through no fault of their own, they have been responsible for the *fad du jour* mentality that often exists in organizations and that often drives their strategic planning processes. The dynamic is typically:

- An article gets published touting the success of an organization or an approach and the article touts a new technique or perspective for managing organizations;

- Managers read the article and take away the concepts and buzzwords and not much more;

- Without doing the hard work of thinking, they begin utilizing the approach in their organization in planning for the future.

I am a huge fan of the HBR, but if you start significant change in your organization based solely on having read an article or a book, you're screwed. If you're going to put resources into an approach, at least you can arrange to spend a week at a company who has done something similar and learn everything you can about four components of the change:

- People

- Organization

- Technology

- Task (Work)

The really good organizations can explain why their approach worked, what it *really* took to make it happen and what didn't work so well or failed.

I've been involved in a number of organizational changes that have received press attention; when the successes are written about there is a Disney-like, Walton Mountain at Christmas Time, Up With People (thanks for that line Dennis Miller) magical spirit to the write-ups. We've all seen how history gets re-written, how failures are someone else's problems and everyone takes credit for successes! Ask the folks on the ground about what really happened and you'll get a completely different, and much more realistic, view of what it takes to make organizational change.

Fad du jour Worksheet

Make a list of management fads that have come and gone in your organization in the past 10 years. Why did they take hold? Why did they fail?

Management Fad	Lessons Learned About Failure

A Brief History of the Practice of Business Strategy

I don't want to leave the impression that *strategic thinking* is new and that it only has value if its part of an organizational process or is wrapped in the terms we'll discuss in this book. I'm sure pre-historic hunters employed strategy and there is even evidence that dogs were domesticated to help with the hunt…the fist example of outsourcing, perhaps?

Military strategy has existed for as long as there have been battles. There have even attempts to apply military strategies to businesses; some have even succeeded from time to time. *The Art of War* by Sun Tzu continues to re-emerge every couple of years as required management reading. The risk here is that managers will apply the lessons of Sun Tzu improperly (e.g., the wrong context) or use the terminology of the book and, in doing so, mask the weakness of their plans. After a while, these managers sound like the Water Cooler Guy from Saturday Night Live…they verbalize a bunch of hip phrases without any connection or understanding to the verbiage.

I'm certain that businesses have had strategies for as long as there have been businesses. Traders in the Middle East and Africa no doubt thought about what products they'd sell, where they'd get them from, whom they'd sell them to, how to price and sell them, etc. They most likely formed *strategic alliances* with suppliers and other traders and thought about defensive strategies for their competitors. I have to believe that these early traders also had strategies for financing their businesses.

I'm also certain that there are many managers who have strategic plans in their heads that are as profound and effective as plans that were created by any team of consultants and managers. One of the most profound strategic plans I've ever seen was drawn on a napkin over breakfast just before heading out for a day's sail.

Let's take a look, however, at the process of strategic planning as it's emerged over time. Surprisingly, formal strategic planning as we think of it today is a relatively new area of study.

The Harvard Policy Model was developed as part of the business policy course taught at the Harvard Business School since the 1920s (Christensen et al. 1983 and earlier versions). The main purpose of the *Harvard model* was to determine the best fit between an organization and its environment through policies and purposes.

Many attribute the work of Bruce Henderson and the Boston Consulting Group with their brilliantly conceived matrix of product strategies as a milestone in modern strategic planning methodologies. If you've ever used the language of *Cash Cow*, *Dog*, *Question Mark* or *Star*, that language is straight from Henderson's work. The following diagram (from QuickMBA.com) shows how BCG's matrix organized products and services based on the growth of the market they are in and their market share.

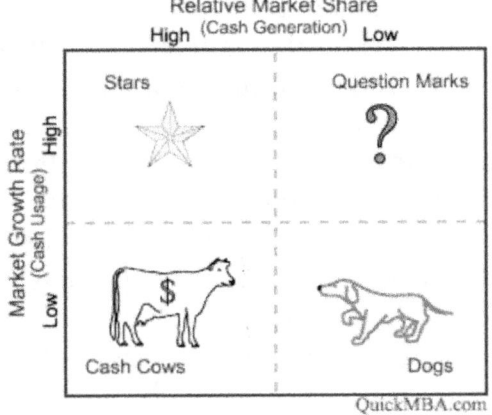

The basic technique involves analyzing and positioning your individual products/services in one of the four quadrants based on their *relative market share* and on the *rate of growth of the market* for that product/service. The dynamic use of the model involves taking cash from products/services in the *Cash Cows* (high market share, low market growth) and *Dogs* (low market share, low market growth) categories and using it to invest in the *Stars* (high market share, high growth) and to fund a selective set of *Question Marks* (low market share, high growth market products/services) opportunities with the intent of turning them into Stars and, eventually, Cash Cows. Dogs, as you might guess, need to be shut down since their going nowhere in a market that's stagnant and in which you have a low market share.

One often-overlooked requirement in utilizing this matrix is a clear understanding of your core competence. It makes no sense to talk about investing in the future of products and services without being aware of the places and ways in which your organization has a strategic advantage due to its unique, defensible core competencies.

However, I have always had a love/hate relationship with *seemingly* easily digested models, such as the BCG matrix, which get applied by well-meaning managers (and consultants) in a formulaic way without any appreciation for the really difficult component of any powerful model…the thinking that has to accompany its use. I have seen the BCG Matrix misused at least as often as I've seen it used appropriately. No model/technique/approach will take the place of critical thinking for an organization and its senior managers. These models can not only inform and guide the thinking of an organization, they can also lull the organization into a false sense of security by believing that the model/matrix is a guarantor that their thinking is correct. Unfortunately, for many organizations, Strategic Planning has turned into the *Clown College* of management work. It is typically done once a year, is based on little or no *meaningful* data (I'm talking about information from customers and the field) or understanding, is typically a staff role where the folks doing the work have to beg for attention and resources and where the apparent *successful outcome* of the strategic planning process is an artifact or document accompanied by a deck of really slick PowerPoint slides.

The next step in this charade is that managers are asked to align their departmental plans with the Strategic Plan; I call this forced alignment *'Agenda Bending'*. Later in this book, we'll look at this common game of bending work to look strategic in a moment.

The Failure Of Strategic Planning

It's possible that you and your organization are an exception to what I've described; in which case you can put this book on your bookshelf or leave it on your desk as a conversation piece. On the other hand, you and many others have bought this book for a reason.

Just to put a finer point on this:

According to the U.S. Small Business Administration, over 50% of small businesses fail in the first year and 95% fail within the first five years. I can think of only two possible reasons for this: wrong strategy or wrong implementation plan. If I had to bet, I'd say the strategy was probably weak and the implementation plan was an afterthought.

But, sadly, it's not only small business that fail due to the lack of a coherent set of strategies:

Almost the entire US Auto Industry with the possible exception of Ford; the genesis of the failure of this industry is the same as the albino kid on the porch in Deliverance (thank you Dennis Miller). They did it to themselves in a well-documented strategy of rapid model design changes, planned obsolescence through terrible quality control and failing to acknowledge the price of fuel rising as they built big, heavy, fuel-inefficient vehicles!

The consumer electronics industry (GE, RCA, Philco, etc.); yes, the companies that owned the living rooms of our grandparents and parents got left in the dust by newer designs, better quality and a dedication to the consumer.

The entire Swiss watch industry…they are primarily boutique lines now and nowhere near dominant except at the very high end of the industry;

The computer industry: Digital Equipment Corporation is a painful example. Note: in the spirit of transparency, I worked at DEC for 14 years. I recently heard Bill Gates speaking at Columbia University and he said that DEC was one of the companies he had admired most in the computer industry when he first started in the business. I'll talk more about DEC later on. Other companies that didn't survive/thrive in the computer industry in spite of being early entrants and having deep pockets? RCA, Data General, Wang, Commodore, Tandy (Radio Shack), Xerox (Star Workstation), Epson, NEC, WordPerfect, Lotus, Olivetti (PC),

I predict that Microsoft is in danger of joining this list as Google, Mozilla, Apple and the open source community (talented computer folks who think software should be free and who create free products similar to software like Word, Excel, PowerPoint, etc.) continue to eat their lunch. Recently Microsoft re-entered the mobile phone software business…they are so far behind Apple and Google in this space that it's almost laughable. As I'm writing this, Microsoft is generating some buzz in the market with Kinetic, a Wii-like game system which doesn't require a hand-held controller and that reads the position of your arms and legs and feeds that information to the game that you're playing.

Immediately after writing this, it was revealed that someone has ported the Kinetic software to other hardware meaning that Microsoft may have lost the ability to own, control (and charge for) the Kinetic capability...and that all happened in less than a week after the release of the product.

Imagine the millions of dollars that went into the development, production and marketing of this break-through market. Imagine the technical expertise at Microsoft's disposal. Now imagine the dismay when, less than a week after this product's release, it is being hacked and, with a little bit of technical acumen, can be ported to other hardware platforms. This would be a good time for you to scratch your head.

The Cost Of Planning Poorly: Companies Who's Planning Processes Failed Them

The following are some examples of companies who didn't get it even close to right…even when they held very strong cards…even when their existing business should've caused them to *trip over* the right answers for sustaining their lead in their industry.

Sony: I've just read where, in 2010, Sony is discontinuing production of the Walkman. This is occurring 9 years after the iPod was introduced. Two questions: why didn't Sony introduce an iMan (I made that up, but you get the point) before Apple entered the market and what the hell were they doing for 9 years? Here's the problem: there was probably a small but steady market for the Walkman until there wasn't. The irony is that Sony's *core competence* has always been *miniaturization*; you know, like how you can get thousands of more songs in a much smaller format by going from a Walkman to an iPod.

Utilizing the product matrix of Bruce Henderson (BCG) Sony could've treated the Walkman as either a Cash Cow or a Dog and could've prescribed pumping money from the Walkman to the development of the iMan, man.

Blockbuster vs. Netflix: OK, another question: which company do you think of when you think of movie rentals. If you're over 40 years old, your answer was probably Blockbuster; under 40, your answer was most likely Netflix.

Netflix is to the movie rental industry what Amazon is to the book industry. Imagine that you're sitting at a Blockbuster strategic planning meeting and someone says 'hey, have you guys seen this new company, Netflix...they rent movies by having customers order over the internet and then, get this, *shipping* the movies through the US Mail.

What *must have* happened based on Blockbusters apparent lack of response to this new competitor, is a vigorous, humor and derision-filled discussion of why Netflix's approach could never work: cannot keep enough inventory, damage to the disks in transit, people won't return them, how much time it takes to get the disks to and from the customer, and so on. Next agenda item: our annual executive gathering in a sun-filled resort.

Too many years later, Blockbuster woke up and devised a brilliant model of being able to order a movie online, receive it by mail and then return it either by mail or in person to your local Blockbuster store. What's wrong with this, you ask?

- Way too late. By the time Blockbuster woke up, Netflix was the generic name for ordering movies online. If you were a Netflix member, you're not likely to bail out of that membership and not likely to join an additional service. Why not you ask...

- Netflix had done something else: not only was this a way to rent movies, it was a way to be social about it and share your film choices and reviews with friends...you can share your list with friends, learn what they really liked, rent it yourself, review it and other friends would benefit. This is commonly called *crowdsourcing* and we'll discuss it more detailed later. Brilliant, fun and once you build up that kind of data about your customers, you're not about to be easily overtaken by competition. This is a classic *new* barrier to competition!

- Finally, and this is probably the trump card that drove Blockbuster into Chapter 11, the future is not physical media…its digital media delivered over the Internet. Netflix, again, saw this coming and is offering tens of thousands of titles to be watch using streaming technology on a computer and they also teamed up with TiVo, Hulu and Boxee. Not familiar with these terms, Google them. Not familiar with Google….it's time to get familiar with the *internet machine* as my father used to call it.

- A significant part of the Netflix story is that it *defined its business as entertainment distribution,* not movie rentals and not mail order…think about how that informed the nature and timing of the strategic decisions that Netflix made. The way a company defines the business its in is a critical *strategic* decision. Now, the question becomes, can Netflix stay in the game? Is there a new strategy being developed by TiVo or the content-owners (movie studios) that will leapfrog the Netflix model?

 Keep these examples in mind as you read the following examples:

Polaroid: Quick, who commercialized instant photography? Need a clue? Go back to the beginning of this paragraph. Do you own a digital camera? Is it a Polaroid? I didn't think so. Again, a perfect example of where a company's strategic planning process completely failed them.

Polaroid was located in about 5 inches from the MIT campus and, clearly, the failure to get into digital photography wasn't due to a lack of technical expertise nearby. I cannot believe that not one senior manager at Polaroid wasn't aware of the approaching digital photography market and, given Polaroid's name and experience in the market of instant photography, they could've leant instant credibility to the concept *and* gained a competitive advantage over companies like Canon, Sony (they get a point for this one) and Kodak....wait, Kodak? Yes, Kodak got digital photography even though they weren't in that exact market; and Polaroid didn't get it? The only ways to explain this are:

- Poor strategic planning.
- Poor market intelligence.
- They defined their business in such a way that involved chemicals and paper *but not* instant photography.
- They listened to the wrong people.

Now, if you're Canon or Kodak and are feeling safe in the digital camera field, consider this: the last 3 times I reached for my digital camera, I put it back on the shelf. Why? My iPhone 4 is more than adequate for 90% of the shots that I want to take and it's always at hand. As photographers say, the best camera is the one you have with you.

Encyclopedia Britannica: Some of you are old enough to remember when the 'go to' source for information was the Encyclopedia Britannica. I still remember the hush that came over our house in the town where I grew up in Central Massachusetts when a salesman for that company paid us a visit...I'm talking about a *house call* here! The salesman convinced my parents that my entire future rested upon their purchasing this set of books *even though we lived right next door to the Public Library*. He sold them a dream.

How does a company go from the primary source of information to essentially nothing but library *eye candy* overnight? Well, it happened in two stages. The first stage was the introduction of Microsoft's Encarta in 1993. This was a DVD with an entire encyclopedia's contents on it, and it contained, in addition to the content of photos and illustrations that you'd expect in a printed encyclopedia, music clips and videos. It seemed absolutely incredible at the time.

Just as Microsoft was feeling very full of themselves over the defeat of the hard copy, paper encyclopedias, they got *their* lunch eaten. Two online sources obliterated any form of encyclopedia that wasn't up-to-the-minute current: Google and Wikipedia.

OK, stop giving me reasons not to trust either source. The reality is, I'll take instantly updated information, which may require some sifting to test for accuracy and a glance as to who the source is and whether I trust it or not, over a book or DVD that was created even 3 months ago.

On a bit of a tangent, newspapers suffer the same problem as every print medium…they can never, ever be as current as their online counterparts…add to the mix the willingness of onsite people to upload stories and photos as they're happening (crowdsourcing!), and you would have to *really love the feel of a newspaper* to choose it for your source of news vs. online content. I would argue that newspapers aren't the source of news anymore; they are a portable way to read what happened in the world yesterday. Now that the Amazon Kindle and Apple iPad have online newspaper content, the portability argument for newspapers is rendered moot.

Zagat Survey: (or the Zagat Guide as most of us call it, if we call it anything) is another study responding to the power of technology way too late…specifically, they missed the internet/smart phone market while there was still time for them to shape and possibly own it.

Zagat was the original crowdsourced source of information about restaurants. Most restaurants of any size and quality showed the Zagat rating and most savvy diners would consult the familiar maroon booklet before choosing a new restaurant and, yet, when it came to making the transition to electronic content, Zagat was apparently out to lunch here's the whole story of where Zagat's online presence ranks:

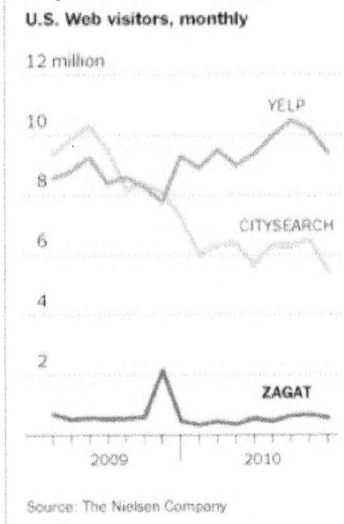

U.S. Web visitors, monthly

Source: The Nielsen Company

As printed in the NY Times on November 14, 2010

The iPhone app for Zagat costs $9.99. The Yelp app, which employs instant crowdsourcing as well as augmented reality, is…wait for it, $0.00, nada, zilch. Who you gonna' go to for your restaurant information? If you're over 50, probably Zagat, until you get an iPhone. If you're under 50, someone may have to tell you what Zagat is! By the way, look at the arc of the curves for Yelp vs. Citysearch…I'd be staying awake at night trying to explain the divergence (if I were Citysearch) and drop in usage (Yelp and Citysearch) in 2010.

digital This next example is painfully personal; I spent 14 years working for Digital Equipment Corporation (DEC). Twelve of those fourteen years were some of the most engaging, fun, meaningful and connected of my career. Some of you may not have heard of DEC, so I'll simply say that at the height of its success, it was second only to IBM in terms of size and, for three straight years, without acquiring another company, the increase in their annual revenues (just the increase, the '*delta*') would've qualified as a Fortune 500 Company…three years in a row! It was such a force in the high tech world that MIT students used to trade and sell anything with a Digital logo on it! DEC's story is very similar to Polaroid's.

DEC was founded in 1957 by an MIT graduate and located its corporate headquarters very close to the MIT Cambridge, MA campus (a few miles down the road in Maynard, MA). Ken Olsen, the revered founder of DEC, conceived the idea of creating a computer architecture that would allow computers to become *departmental* computers located close to the users rather than the existing paradigm of that time of huge, monolithic (IBM) computers which resided in glassed-in *inner sanctums* accessible by a very few people.

The term used for these smaller, departmental computers was 'mini-computer' and they were a huge hit! The mini-computers were smaller, faster, easier to use, much cheaper alternatives to anything else on the market.

In 1987 I can remember standing near a bank of pay phones during DECWorld, a 2 week marketing effort showing only DEC products to customers who traveled from all over the world *at their own expense*, listening to senior managers, seemingly one after another, yelling into the phones something like 'I don't care what you've told IBM, get out here tomorrow and see what DEC is doing, it's amazing!'

Okay, now work with me here. The company which was founded by a technologist, who's model of computing was to go from large to smaller, the company known for it's incredible technical expertise, the company that was the darling of Wall Street and the envy of everyone in the industry, no longer exists! What could possibly go wrong?

You're going to think I'm making this up…just as Polaroid didn't see digital cameras as part of the business they were in, DEC (specifically Ken Olsen, the founder) saw *engineering workstations* (one step smaller than departmental mini-computers) and, then most critically *personal computers* (one step smaller than engineering workstations) as irrelevant until it was too late…and then Digital implemented the strategy for catching up in both markets they did it in a very flawed way.

Rather than building hardware that ran industry standard software (operating system and applications such as Microsoft, Lotus, WordPerfect, etc.for PCs), DEC chose to build PCs that ran only proprietary DEC software. My son Jason, who was 12 years old at the time accompanied me one weekend to help me set up some of the new Digital PCs in a learning lab to help employees master this new way of computing. When he learned of the proprietary nature of the software he said 'Dad, this is really dumb!' I had no choice but to agree with him. Twelve years old!

Rather than focusing its sizeable engineering and manufacturing talent in the PC Market, DEC chose to sink huge amounts of the company's resources into going in the *other* direction in attempting to build larger, more powerful super computers…you know, suspiciously like the old IBM mainframes that the company crushed when it created the mini computer. You can't make this stuff up!

Need another quick example of what happens when strategy doesn't keep up with reality? Consider the Swiss watch market…common lore has it that when the digital watch was invented, it was brought to the Swiss who looked at and muttered (in Swiss), "WTF, its not even a watch". Do your own market research today and notice how many of the watches you see today are Swiss analogs vs. digital watches.

Garmin: I mentioned that I don't take my digital camera with me much anymore due to the camera in my iPhone. Well, Garmin and other dedicated GPS manufacturers are also being sideswiped. During my last three business trips, rather than tote my Garmin GPS with me, I simply cranked up my iPhone and it guided me to my appointments. Apps such as Waze, which are free and count on crowdsourcing for up to the minute traffic reports as well as being able to enter your contacts for destination addresses rather than entering them to the GPS, and are already eating away at the market share of Garmin and other GPS manufacturers. A larger number of people have stopped buying dedicated GPSs in favor of software for the smartphone. Below is a screen shot from Waze showing the crowdsourced, real-time traffic feature.

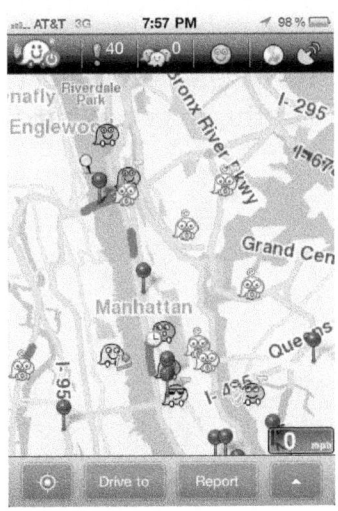

What's been Garmin's response to this flurry of activity? This:

About $450

...no, it's <u>*not*</u> an iPhone, it's a Garmin GPS. At the time of this writing it costs $450.00 and the one feature that it has going for it is speech recognition...you can talk to it. Well, the problem is that the iPhone has speech recognition capability for other apps and it's just a matter of time until someone comes up with an app that will compete with the Garmin in the speech recognition space....for about 1/10th the cost and without the need for another piece of hardware.

Mental Exercise: The Garmin Strategy Home Game

If you were creating future strategies for Garmin, what would you do?

- **What would be your definition of the business you're in?**

- **What are your core competencies?**

- **How would you use what you have to compete in the future?**

- **What wouldn't you do?**

Barnes & Noble: In addition to the battle for e-readers that I describe below, Barnes & Noble also had their lunch eaten by Amazon in their core business: book sales. In 2007 Amazon soared past Barnes & Noble book sales and as Amazon's sales revenue continues to increase, Barnes & Noble's revenue is declining in this core business. One of the primary reasons Amazon is going to be hard to match in terms of customer loyalty is their interesting use of *crowdsourcing*. I remember the first time I received a *recommendation* from Amazon for a new book by one of my favorite authors I was stunned. Based on a previous purchase, Amazon's database was on the lookout for books by the same author and, even, books on the same or related topics. I realized I had passively crowdsourced their database, it was specific to me and that Barnes & Noble was screwed…they didn't know what books I had purchased and had no way of finding out; Amazon owned me. I jumped on the opportunity to purchase the new book from Amazon and further fed the Amazon.com growth curve.

The Confusing Example Of Barnes & Noble: Too Late, Too Soon And Then Too Late

To further disabuse you that Strategic Planning can be formulaic and that it is in any way easy, consider Barnes & Noble again, the former largest book retailer in the United States: they were beaten to the punch in online book sales by Amazon.com and then, to make matters even worse, *they* beat Amazon.com to the market with an electronic book reader in the late nineties. A combination of bad luck (they formally released it on September 11, 2001) combined with less than state-of-the art technology and hobbled by a less than vigorous participation by publishers caused B&N to yank the product in 2003.

In 2007, Amazon introduced the Kindle. Since then, B&N has introduced the Nook and the two companies are locked in a price war and they both now have Apple's iPad (not a hygiene product in spite of its name) to contend with.

Instead of Barnes & Noble *owning* the online and e-book markets, they are running a poor second (and perhaps 3rd if we consider Apple's iPad forays into this market) due to being too late online and too soon with too little in e-books. I know, right, this truly is difficult terrain, this strategy stuff. Buck up, we're going to drive through this together.

Here's a photo of a Barnes & Noble store on the Upper West Side of New York City late on a Sunday morning in mid-November 2010; if you listen, you can hear yourself think:

Concerned that perhaps I had unfairly chosen a point in time that the Nook counter was empty, a week later, I was at another Barnes & Noble in NYC on Black Friday (the Friday after Thanksgiving) and the scene was essentially the same.

Below, on the other hand, is a photo of Apple Store on Fifth Avenue in Manhattan on typical day:

Now, admittedly, this is not data but even if you could argue that Amazon's Kindle is the logical competition for the Nook, Barnes & Noble was so late coming into the market with a serious product that it opened up a spot for another contender, Apple's iPad, which most-likely will take at least 2nd place in the e-book reader market due to it's greater general functionality.

Mental Exercise: The Barnes & Noble Strategic Planning Home Game

If you were creating future strategies for Barnes & Noble, what would you do?

- **What would be your definition of the business you're in?**

- **What are your core competencies?**

- **How would you use what you have to compete in the future?**

- **What wouldn't you do?**

Avoiding The Abyss Worksheet

What Does *Your Organization* Have In Common With The Lessons From These Companies:

Organization	Similarities	Dissimilarities	Lessons
Sony Walkman			
Blockbuster			
Polaroid			
Encyclopedia Britannica			
Zagat			
Digital Equipment Corp.			
Swiss Watches			
Garmin & GPS Industry			
Barnes & Noble			

The Thinking Behind Bad Plans

Often, there is no *strategic* thinking behind Strategic Plans. More often than not, the plans I see appear to be written in the following way:

- Look in the rear view mirror to see what the organization has been doing and declare that they'll do more of it;

- Increase/decrease the relevant *historical* factors by some arbitrary percent:

    o Increase sales by x%

    o Decrease costs by y%

    o Penetrate new markets by z%

    o Etc.

- Based on the % growth targets above, build elaborate spreadsheets showing the new business model; the problem is, that this approach is similar to the opening line of Kafka's *Metamorphosis* "When Gregor Samsa woke from troubled dreams, he found himself transformed in his bed into a terrible vermin." Once you accept the opening sentence, the rest of the book makes total sense. When planning is done by making assumptions or setting goals without strategies to achieve them, the success of those plans is predicated on accepting (as opposed to planning for) the first assumptions, e.g., *we will increase sales by 15%*.

- Create a plan which grows your overhead, span of control and make sure that it *appears* to be in alignment with the Strategic Plan via *Agenda Bending* (more later) which, for the most part, no one takes very seriously;

- Create a plan that *sucks up* to senior management's favorite initiatives or buzz phrases du jour.

- Copy another organization's strategy with the rationale 'hey, we're in the same or similar businesses'. I call this the Bartender's Tattoo Gambit...

The photo shown here is of an actual tattoo on the actual arm of an actual New York City bartender. When asked about it, he told us the following story.

Apparently he'd always wanted a tattoo, but his mother was dead-set against it. She threatened to beat the hell out of him if he ever considered getting one. Then, one day in a flash of brilliance, he formed what he thought was the perfect strategy: he would get the exact same tattoo that his beloved grandfather had gotten while in the Navy, specifically, the frigate you see featured in photo above.

His plan involved revealing the tattoo at the next family gathering while his mother *and* grandfather would be seated at the same dining room table along with a large number of other relatives. His thinking was that he would reveal his new adornment as an *homage* to his grandfather and, even if his mother was horrified, she would have to pretend to be impressed that the bartender had gotten inked as a tribute to his grandfather.

The day arrived, Thanksgiving I believe, and the bartender waited until most of the meal had been consumed. He then clinked his glass to get the attention of the assembled crowd including his mother and grandfather. He announced with great flourish that he wanted to show them something that he'd recently done as a tribute to his grandfather's years of service in the Navy. He then proceeded to roll up his sleeve revealing the tattoo on his arm.

His mother was horrified and made no secret about her horror. The bartender countered with something like 'how can you be so cold, this is in tribute to my grandfather's years of service to his country'.

Mom then countered with 'You're both a**holes; your grandfather was never in the Navy and got that tattoo one drunken night in Houston'…and she stormed out of the room.

The moral of this story: you shouldn't copy your competitor's or anyone else's strategy since you have no idea why they got *their* tattoo…and you might end up really pissing off your mom in the process. Strategies are not *one size fits all*. They work for specific organizations for specific reasons, not the least of which are the specific core competencies of those organizations and how they've been leveraged to gain a strategic advantage.

This isn't to say that you shouldn't look at other organizations and their strategies; you *can* learn a lot from other organizations and from other industries.

If, on the other hand, you aren't able to create a solid strategic plan for your company, then find someone who can.

The Thinking Behind Good Plans

Good Plans Will Address Explicitly:

- The Vision for the organization.

- The organization's core competencies. This is no place for platitudes. You say you are good at customer relations? How do you know? Can you prove it? How?

- How you will engage customers and the field.

- Your intended position in the market? Some options:

    o Low price (generics, McDonald's)

    o High functionality (iPhone, Mac, MS Office, etc.)

    o Convenience (gas stations mini-stores – I know I love combining my petro-chemicals with a cup 'o coffee and a Twinkie);

    o High-end, high price (Gucci, Bentley, etc.)

- How you will establish your brand such that it creates and solidifies your position in the market.

- How you can create a future for your organization that leverages both your core competencies *and* builds upon those strengths such that you have a *sustainable* competitive advantage with significant barriers to entry for your competition.

- How you will sequence and stage your strategies and tactics such that they support, enable and leverage each other as opposed to simply listing them without any sense of the integration between them. The risk in not doing this is that the strategies/tactics could easily fight and cannibalize each other (resources, market awareness, brand formation, etc.).

- How you will implement the plan given your culture, resources, skills and current workload.

- How you will get feedback as to whether the plan is still valid given changes to the environment and learnings from implementation.

The Architecture Of Mission, Vision, Strategies, Tactics Objectives and Goals: The Dream Team's OJ Simpson Defense

I have a love/hate relationship with the following example. I created it a few years ago, out of desperation, as a way for organizations to see what the hierarchy of terms looks like in action and to give them a diagnostic tool with which to assess their Strategic Plans. Why do I love it? It *always* works with clients in a way that endless definitions and discussions do not. Invariably they will identify that they have no Strategy layer in their plans. Why do I hate it? It's the OJ trial and *everyone* has an opinion regarding his guilt or innocence. They tend to get hooked. Let's take a look:

The Inferred OJ Defense Strategy

Mission	Vision	Strategies	Tactics	Objectives	Goals
Get OJ Acquitted	Successful, Career-Enhancing (for attorneys) Defense	Establish Reasonable Doubt re: OJ's Ability To Commit Crime	Challenge Evidence	Collection, Contamination, Analysis	5 Expert Witnesses
			Argue Conspiracy	LAPD Motive, 'Rush To Judgment'	Racism, No Other Suspects
			Leverage Distrust: LAPD	Portray as Inept & Racist	Handling Of Evidence, Furman
			Show Others Had Motive	Drug Deal Gone Bad, Faye Resnick	Show Nicole's Lifestyle
		Challenge Quality Of The Evidence	Leverage 'Dream Team'	Power Team At The Table	Always 3 – 4 Lawyers Visible
			Influence Jury Externally	Media To Influence Juror's Families	2 News Conf. 2 TV Appears.

The diagram above is meant to illustrate how each of the component parts of planning the OJ Defense Strategy fit together and support each other. The *'aha moment'* for clients usually comes when they realize that their entire strategic plan is almost entirely to the right of the diagram in the areas of *objectives and goals* and that the organization does not have a set of *strategies (and sometimes tactics)* similar to the OJ example's 'Establish Reasonable Doubt re: OJ's Ability To Commit Crime' and 'Challenge Quality Of The Evidence'.

Worksheet: Checking The Structure Of Your Plan Compared To The OJ Example

Show how your company's strategies, tactics & objectives map against the OJ example.

Mission:

Vision:

Strategies:

Tactics:

Objectives:

Definition of Terms

I'll try to not make this section too academic, but I think it's important that we more precisely define the terms that I've been using in this book. If you don't like the following definitions, or your organization uses a different set, create/define your own. Be sure to communicate the operative definitions with your organization and be sure to use them consistently. I'll provide *my* hierarchy below since I find this can vary by organization. Regardless of how you define your terms, if a significant part of your lexicon and process doesn't include critical thinking about what business you're in, what your organization is good at (*core competence*) and *how* you will use that knowledge to create a sustainable *strategic advantage*, then you're screwed. As you'll see, *Strategic Planning* is about creating a path from where you are to where you want to be.

The terms, in hierarchical, descending order of scope and ascending order of detail, are Mission ->Vision->Strategies->Tactics->Objectives->Goals:

- **Mission: Definition**– what is the organization's purpose for being? Although broad in scope, the Mission should relate directly to your organization and inspire those who will work towards achieving it. Here's one I don't like; it's from a Toyota dealership in New York: "To be an innovative industry leader totally committed to customer satisfaction, employee satisfaction, integrity and teamwork". What's not to like?

    o Well, for starters it doesn't even mention automobiles which is the business they're in! Actually, I bought a car from them, they have a gigantic **Toyota** sign in front of their building and I just assumed they were in the business of selling them…I'll have to Google them!

o   The Toyota dealer's Mission Statement doesn't say anything that is specific to their industry, region or dealership.

o   The other problem is that it's difficult to imagine what any particular employee would do differently on Monday morning after reading this…it is just a collection of important sounding words.

Contrast the Toyota dealer's attempt at a Mission Statement with that of Hyundai; In 2000, the chairman of Hyundai challenged the company achieve the top level of quality in the industry within five years. It's specific, measureable and provides meaningful direction to the organization about what it should be achieving. I'll talk more about what else Hyundai did to improve their quality; a Mission Statement is simply not enough!

One particular Mission Statement which is often held up as a model is John F. Kennedy's "I believe that this nation should commit itself to achieving the goal, before this decade is out, of landing a man on the moon and returning him safely to the earth". It's considered a model because:

o   It is specific – he could've chosen something akin to 'becoming a leader in space exploration', but instead narrowed down the mission to a specific, large audacious target for the decade to come;

○ It defines a significant *stretch* for the organization as well as defining what the organization will be about;

○ It has a time dimension;

○ It informs every person involved in this effort in a way that shaped their every day work and long range plans; if a program didn't in some way support the Mission, it was either dropped or given a lower priority than those that were in direct support of the Mission.

This diagram is meant to illustrate the levels of thinking that follow and how they relate to each other; the message here is that Vision should *inform* Strategy and Strategy should *inform* Tactics.

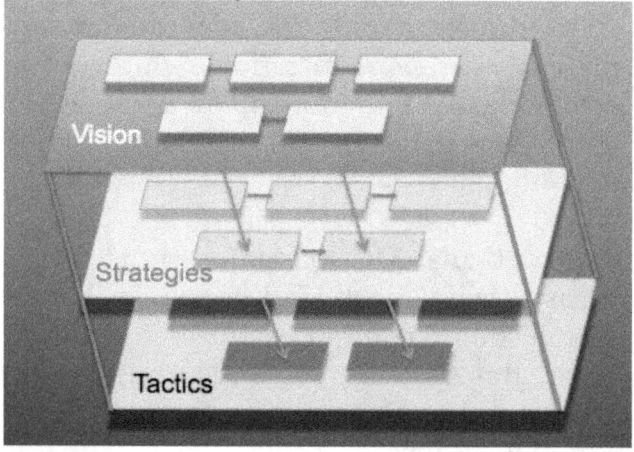

- **Vision: Definition** - Given the Mission of the organization, what are *this particular organization's* specific aspirations for the future; what does it want to become, what does it want to do? As I mentioned earlier, we shouldn't confuse Vision with *Vision Statement*; they sound similar, but most Vision

Statements were created by a group of weary managers, sitting in a remote location, trying to *wordsmith* language that all could agree with so that they could get back to their real lives. We also see the dynamic where one person takes it as an action item to write the Vision Statement, circulates it to his/her colleagues and:

- o People immediately embrace it because it means ending the charade of non-productive work;

- o People engage in a semantic smack-down that lasts for months.

My experience with Vision Statements is that they're usually the result of *wars of attrition* where the people with the most time, loudest voices or threatening behavior (passive or aggressive) win the game of getting their version of a Vision Statement adopted by the group.

When I use the word *Vision*, I am referring to a shared understanding of where the organization is going in the next 5 – 10 years. It will include such information as:

- How will the organization's work, structures and processes enable the Mission to be accomplished; this is not a plan for achieving the mission, but more of an *architecture for achieving the vision*. If we were building a house, this would be the architect's rendering of what the finished house would look like.

- What businesses the company will be in; which businesses will it *not* be in. *Note*: I dedicate a whole

section in this book to this seemingly simple
question of *What Business(es) Are You In*.

- In its chosen businesses, what are the core
  competencies of the organization and how will
  those be leveraged;

- What markets (products, services, geographic
  locations, virtual presence, socio-economic sector,
  ethnic, etc.) will the organization operate in;

- What will be the nature of the relationships between
  the organization and:

    o   Customers;

    o   Employees;

    o   Suppliers;

    o   Competitors;

    o   Regulators;

    o   Etc.

- What will the overall process and value-added
  chain look like including what the organization will
  do itself and what it will partner with or outsource
  to others.

- Other components of the overall *architecture* of the
  Vision that will convey the future to the
  organization.

- **Strategies: Definition** – Given the Vision for the future, *what path* will the organization follow to get there? Well you knew we'd get to crunch time in terms of my finally having to offer a definition of **strategic**. I'm going to offer a number of examples here as a way to *surround* the topic and then offer my working definition. My hope is that one or more of these examples will act as a definition for you without having to corner you into accepting only an academic definition of the concept. Here goes:

  o I believe this first example comes from Regis McKenna, consulting guru to many high tech firms, notably Apple. The **strategy** employed by Word Processing software vendors was based on creating a *pull* for the product by introducing word processing into the *legal departments* of large corporations. The thinking was:

    ▪ Legal departments had natural demands for the functionality of word processing (a ton of text as well as boiler plate-intensive processes);

    ▪ Every organization of any size has a legal department;

    ▪ Once 'Legal' began using word processing within organizations, the other departments: Purchasing, Sales, Manufacturing, etc., would *pull* on the technology so that they could utilize it themselves.

- Once large legal departments had access to word processing, smaller firms who did business with them would *pull* on the technology as well.

- You can compare this to other approaches they might have chosen including *pushing* information to all departments through marketing (at great expense) in all companies of a certain size and in a certain industry.

○ **Google**: Another example of how strategic thinking can be used to great competitive advantage is Google. Google was criticized for years for offering their search services for free. The following appeared in the Wall Street Journal in December of 2000:

Limited Business. But how will Google ever make money? There's the rub. The company's adamant refusal to use banner or other graphical ads eliminates what is the most lucrative income stream for rival search engines. Although Google does have other revenue sources, such as licensing and text-based advertisements, the privately held company's business remains limited compared with its competitors'.

The problem was, the Wall Street Journal had no idea what Google's *real strategy* was. I'll offer it a nutshell: Google's *strategy* is (and was) to give away world class search capability as a mechanism to attract *eyeballs* (the buzz term for how many people visit your site) thereby providing an environment within which to sell advertising space in the form of AdWords.

The other component of Google's *strategy* involved offering services to individuals (usually free), make them robust through use by millions of individual users and then offer these products to businesses (usually for a fee).

Many of Google's products look suspiciously like Microsoft's Office Suite, browser and, recently, operating system in direct competition with Windows! The difference in Google's approach is that this is a *cloud* model where the software would *not* reside on your desktop, but on the Internet (*the cloud*).

Notice what both the word processing and the Google examples have in common in terms of *strategy*: they both contain more than one step, a precursor or set of precursors, if you will, which provide the energy and dynamic for getting to their end state vision.

Given these examples and the way in which I use the term with clients, I offer as a definition of Strategy:

A macro-level path or plan describing *how* an organization will get from its current state to its desired state (as expressed in its *Vision*) which shows the interdependence and relationships between the various components of that path or plan, impact on the market and competitors and is in harmony with the environment within which the organization operates.

The following is an analogous definition put into *military terms* which offers the same perspective in terms of linkage of tactics:

Strategy, a word of **military** origin, refers to a plan of action designed to achieve a particular **goal**. In **military usage** strategy is distinct from **tactics**, which are concerned with the conduct of an engagement, while strategy is concerned with how different engagements are linked. How a battle is fought is a matter of tactics: the terms and conditions that it is fought on and whether it should be fought at all is a matter of strategy, which is part of the four levels of warfare: political goals or **grand strategy**, strategy, **operations**, and tactics.

(Beatrice Heuser, The Evolution of Strategy: Thinking War from Antiquity to the Present (Cambridge University Press, 2010), **ISBN 978-0-521-19968-1**, p.27f.) as cited by Wikipedia.com

- **Tactics: Definition** – Tactics are the *specific steps* an organization will take to implement its Strategic Plan. In my experience, most strategic plans enter at this level of the hierarchy without having defined the organization's Mission, Vision or Strategies. There are a couple of problems with this as the entry point:

    o Without Strategy, there is no *context* for tactics; put another way, what are the tactics meant to achieve and how do they relate to each other?

    o The tactics, not having a relationship with a macro-level plan, usually do not have a relationship with each other either. Tactics, absent a Strategic Plan, will often counteract each other or miss the opportunity to leverage each other. One way to think about this issue is to think of an All Star basketball team. What we often see is that, in spite of each player's considerable skills and talents, the team just doesn't gel as a team. So it is with tactics; unless there's an explicit connection between them, they will not deliver what your organization desires.

  Once an organization *gets* the idea of strategies driving tactics, we often see a significant change in perspective including a much more realistic view of what it's going to take to implement their strategic plan.

- **Objectives: Definition** – Given the Strategies, what are the objectives you'll have to achieve to implement them? Think of objectives as milestones that will have to be met if the Mission, Vision and Strategies are to be achieved. The idea of *objectives* in the military sense: our objective is to take control of hill **2542y** within three days. You can imagine that this objective would be part of a set of objectives for a military campaign resulting in achieving a set of tactics in support of an overall strategy. Similarly, an objective for Google might have been to *capture 50% of the search engine traffic worldwide by 2005* and that would be in service of the larger Vision and Strategic Plan.

- **Goals: Definition** – Within each Objective, *goals* represent intermediate milestones on the way to achieving objectives. Back to the Google example: their goal for the next 5 years is to capture 10%, 20% 25%, 35% and 50% search engine traffic respectively. You can see how these goals would then lead to the *objective* above of reaching 50% of the search engine traffic by 2005 and that would be in service of their larger strategy.

Crowdsourcing & The Impact Of Technology: There's a term that I have used and will use a number of times in this book that deserves definition: *crowdsourcing*. This term is used to describe processes wherein responsibility for providing content is left primarily to the users of a product or service. What? If you've looked at user reviews on Amazon.com, read the reviews of a restaurant on Yelp.com or looked up something on Wikipedia.com, you're already familiar with the concept of *crowdsourcing* since the content for this information comes from the users of these websites. This is the modern version of when you'd call your dad (or mom) to ask for a recommendation for a new car or a mechanic.

Why am I focusing on this particular term and type of content? Crowdsourcing has become one of the most powerful ways to offer value to customers *and* develop customer loyalty that is available to strategists today. Once customers/users have invested hours of populating one of these sites with opinions and reviews, or once their personal history is available to make future recommendations (as with Amazon), they're not about to switch to another environment *unless* another site comes along and offers more value! And right there, folks, is why strategic planning is so challenging: if you offer something that is easily duplicated (the buzz term for this these days is *fungible*), you will have your lunch eaten by a competitor. The sad news is that the more successful you are in *your* strategy, the more likely someone will want into the market.

This idea of crowdsourcing has introduced another dynamic which strategists need to factor in to their plans: customer experience and loyalty. Jeff Bezos, the founder of Amazon recently said on Charlie Rose's TV show that the ability of people to share opinions about products with millions of people around the world has changed where organizations need to put their resources. In the past, Bezos explained, companies would invest significant resources in 'shouting about' their product and fewer resources on improving it.

Now, because of crowdsourcing of opinions and reviews, successful organizations focus a much greater portion of their resources on improving the product and customer experience because they know if they do, the conversation about that product in online forums will be positive; failure to have good products has just the reverse effect...people will talk about the shortcomings of their product and recommend other products instead.

A recent use of crowdsourcing has been to engage many people (the crowd) in the design of products. Such sites as Kickstarter.com and Quirky.com bring together product ideas, solicit funding to develop those ideas and utilize the design expertise of users from all over the world who provide input and are rewarded financially for their contributions.

Definition of Terms Worksheet

In the space below show your organization's hierarchy of terms (in descending order) from Mission through Goals/Objectives and, in the next section, provide your organization's shared definitions for these terms. Is the hierarchy used consistently? Are these terms understood and applied consistently by all who use them? If not, what can be done to solve that problem?

Illustrate The Hierarchy Of Terms For Your Organization (Mission, Vision, Strategies, Goals, Objectives)

Define The Terms You Used Above

Breaking The Cycle Of Meaningless Strategic Planning

If their current strategic planning processes are left unaddressed, organizations can expect to continue to go through the motions of strategic planning with correspondingly disappointing results.

Here is what it will take for *your* organization to build a Strategic Planning Process that will actually deliver value:

- Senior management must take this effort seriously; forget about what they espouse, are they willing to participate in the process in an authentic and on-going basis and will they take steps to overcome the certain organizational resistance to the implementation of the plan? Occasionally I'll take on a senior manager in an executive coaching assignment. Invariably these managers will say that they want to be more strategic; by this they mean, spend less time on operational/managerial issues and more time thinking about and implementing strategies. Most are sincere about this desire but, based on my experience, most senior managers define themselves and their success in terms of *doing*, not *thinking*. It takes a willingness for managers to risk spending their time thinking rather than doing, to leave their comfort zones, in order for this transition from operations to strategic thinking to occur. Some make it; most do not.

- Responsibility for the *quality and overall implementation* of the process should be reside with CEO, _not_ the Strategic Planning department;

- If someone other than the CEO is going to manage the process, that someone *must* be an opinion leader and have enough political/organizational clout to make the process real, comprehensive and that person must see it through to implementation; this does not let the CEO off the hook, by the way; he or she still *owns* making this happen!

- Reliance upon data is a double-edged sword:

    o An organization cannot make good decisions without good data;

    o An over-reliance upon data, also known as *analysis paralysis,* will bring the process to its knees; some of the best data an organization can obtain, is carefully understood anecdotal information from customers and the filed.

    o Bring in the folks closest to the customer and closest to the technology...share the plan and *listen* to them without being defensive!

The Failure Of Strategic Thinking Worksheet

List organizations from your industry that fell from a position of prominence/dominance due to a lack of coherent strategies and what could your organization can learn from them:

Failed/Diminished Organization	Lessons For Your Organization

A Diagnostic Test For Your Organization's Strategic Plan

Here's a quick set of checks that you can run to determine whether your organization has a viable strategic plan or not:

- Does the process and implementation involve senior management, especially the CEO and do they share a commitment to execute the Strategic Plan?

- Does your executive team have a working (as opposed to academic) definition for what's *strategic* and what's not? Chances are you have spent endless hours wrapped in discussions about what *strategic* means and are still no closer to understanding it or agreeing to a shared definition. . *Note: having the best [people] [products] [processes] [etc.] is not a strategy. These are outcomes from having good strategies. I can't tell you how many times I've seen strategies stated this way. Makes me want to weep!*

- Do you have a commonly shared *Vision* for the organization or just a *Vision Statement* that looks like every one of your competitors' vision statements? Sub-test: if your Vision Statement is written on a wallet-sized card that you pull out of your pocket every time the Vision Statement comes up in a meeting (usually once a year) you probably are screwed. If your Vision Statement contains mostly consultant-speak buzz phrases such as: ecosystem, extensible, scalable, integrated, customer-centric, best in class, employer of choice, etc., you probably need to revisit it after reading this book. Later, I'll provide a method for creating a Vision.

- Is your Strategic Plan really about *Strategy* or does the plan consist primarily of goals and objectives (i.e., the specific *what* you want to accomplish)? Strategy deals with the how you'll achieve your Vision and, once you're clear on your strategies, the goals and objectives should deal with the *what* you'll need to do and in what order to accomplish your strategic plan.

- Does your plan address scenarios for the future in terms of what could happen to the environment in which your company operates (economy, transformational technologies, competitive trends, legislation, etc.) or does it assume that all of these factors will remain constant for the next 5 to 10 years?

- Does your plan *authentically* address:

  o Your organization's *core competence/core assets*? If your core competence sounds something like 'the best people' or 'caring people' or 'customer driven' then you're probably deluding yourself and relying upon safe, *mom and apple pie* platitudes that you developed late during a weekend retreat just so that you could get back home before the weekend was totally ruined. I'll talk more about what I mean by these terms later on.

  o An understanding of how your core competence/core assets will *translate* into:

    - Demand from the marketplace;

- A profitable business model;

- A barrier to entry for your competitors so that they don't offer a 'me too' product or service next month;

- A sustainable path to the Vision extending out at least five years?

  o An authentic, truthful and brutally honest assessment of your competition, their plans for the future as well as an honest assessment of their competitive advantage? There seem to be two extremes when it comes to this step: organizations either minimize their competitors' strengths or they elevate then to the level of myth. Either approach will cause problems in putting together a successful strategy.

- Does your plan address the impact, specifically, on technology on your industry and on your company? Oh, you don't think technology will play a role in the future of your industry? Great, put the book down and schedule another round of golf; you're so screwed!

- Do your people understand and manage to the plan?

  o Have they been taken on the journey of the thinking leading up to the plan and the strategic choices that were made and why?

  o Have they been included in a meaningful way in the planning process and has their input been solicited?

> o Do they agree with the plan and have they committed to managing to it?

Have you built in rapid feedback loops to see whether:

> o You're following the plan;
>
> o The plan is working as designed;
>
> o There have been shifts in either the internal or external landscapes that need to be factored in to the plan.

Strategic Plan Diagnostic Worksheet

Note: the terms and concepts below are explained in this book if you find that you're not familiar with them look them up.

What is your organization's Mission?

What is its Vision?

What business(es) is your organization in?

What role does your CEO and other senior managers play in planning and implementation?

What are your Core Competencies (see the section on Core Competencies before answering)?

What is the *Design Center* of your strategic plan (see the section on Design Center before answering)?

What are the dynamics of the plan (how do the parts of the plan reinforce and enable each other)?

Are your strategies expressed clearly and logically? Do they integrate into a systemic whole?

Given the strategies, what are the associated tactics that will achieve them?

Does your plan address dependencies and risks?

What is the plan to implement?

Since much of the success of your organization is a function of how well you match up against your competitors, it is critical that you perform a parallel analysis of you key competitors.

Analysis Of Competition Worksheet

From what you know about your top three competitors:

What is their Mission and Vision?

What business(es) are your competitors in?

What are *their* Core Competencies?

What is the *Design Center* of *their* strategic plan?

What are the dynamics of *their* plan?

What are your competitors' tactics and how can you counteract them?

How does their plan match them up against your organization as a competitor? What weaknesses are they attacking?

Note: You'll find detailed guides to many of the following items in the section: *Creating Your Strategic Plan – A Step by Step Guide*

Outline For A Typical Strategic Plan

1. *Introduction*: A paragraph or two to set the stage for why the plan was created, why now, who was involved and any options for people to input to it.

2. *Executive Summary*: Write this assuming that this is all most of your audience will actually read (even if you believe that everyone will read the whole document); force yourself to highlight the critical components of the plan simply and illustrate with simple graphics where possible. This sounds easier than it is in practice; you're attempting to take a large, complex plan and boil it down to a few, readable and engaging pages.

3. *The Plan Itself*:

    a. Environmental Scan: What is the current competitive, technical, economic, geographic, etc. arena within which the organization operates and what trends that are revealing themselves?

b. A definition of what businesses the organization is in.

c. Mission of the organization.

d. Vision of the organization (stated both as text and graphics).

e. A definition of the organization's core competencies and an explanation of how they will be used to develop a sustainable competitive advantage.

f. Explanation of the *Design Center* for the strategic plan.

g. Explanation of the dynamics of the plan in terms of why doing 'a' will enable 'b' and leverage 'c'.

h. Definition of the strategies with more detail.

i. Explanation of the dependencies and risks.

j. Next steps in the process including implementation planning.

Creating Your Strategic Plan – A Step by Step Guide

What follows is the process for creating a plan. The order of these steps is slightly different than the order shown in the Outline above. The reason for this is that the order in which you'll think about the plan is different than the order that you choose to present the plan. Also, if you do not have the experience or skills to facilitate these steps, I've written another book entitled "*No More Meetings From Hell*" which talks about in detail how to facilitate this work.

Step 1. Defining The Business You're In

This step has two characteristics that make it particularly important:

- Everyone *believes* that, not only do they know which business they're in, but they are convinced that there is universal agreement amongst their colleagues on this topic;

- The answer to this question of what business your organization is in is not only difficult to answer for most organizations, but answering it (right or wrong) provides a critical perspective which will drive the future of the organizations through large and small decisions

- The penultimate, somewhat threadbare, example of how to talk about the risks in defining the business you're in is the Buggy Whip Exercise. I'd hesitate to even mention it, except it is useful as an introduction to the topic of defining your business. If you're unfamiliar with this old chestnut, it goes like this:

The **Buggy Whip** *It's 1900. You are the owner of a company that manufactures Buggy Whips. Now, list as many ways as you can to define the business you're in. When I've done this exercise with clients, the list usually contains such things as: buggy whips, whips, motivational devices (I swear that one comes up a frightening number of times), leather goods and the illustrative answer, 'transportation'. The reason 'transportation' is such a good answer is, first of all, the other answers are as about as imaginative as a conversation with TV Talkshow host, Larry King. The other reason is that it's the only answer that would allow the Buggy Whip manufacturer to not only survive when automobiles arrived on the market, but to actually thrive if they got into that segment of the market early enough. Products such as auto seats, seat covers, bumpers, steering wheel and shifter covers and, yes, even tires would've been natural to consider as part of the company's portfolio.*

So, what business is *your* organization in? Here are some examples to help you with your thinking:

- **United States Postal Service:** The worst answer I've ever heard to this question of what business you're in was from a senior executive at the US Postal Service. We were sitting next to each other at a technology conference and, even though email and the World

Wide Web were in their nascent stages, it was clear that communicating electronically was going to be huge. With that it mind, and in the context of the conversation we were having about business planning, I asked him how the US Postal Service defined the business it was in. He didn't hesitate, suggesting that he had in fact thought about this before, 'Oh, that's easy, we deliver the mail'. I gasped. The amount of snail mail I receive has declined steadily over the past 5 years and even the obligatory monthly bills now come to me electronically allowing me to view and pay them from anywhere in the world. I love the irony that the Mail application on the Mac uses a postage stamp as an icon…I guess it's because they deliver the mail! So, what business do you think the US Postal Service is in or should be in?

• **Media:** TV networks and stations, newspapers, magazines, the film and recording industries and even book publishers are facing the perils of getting this answer wrong. The question they are struggling with is '*how should we produce our product given the overwhelming capability of today's technology*'. It seems that the *better* question would be: *how are people going to view, read, share and listen to content in the future and how can we carve out a profitable stake in that business*? The answer to that will provide a much sharper answer to the question 'what business are we in?' I recently heard Gary Trudeau, the creator of the comic strip Doonesbury, comment that he feels that the days of newspapers are limited which, for him is especially vexing since his work appears primarily in newspapers. When asked whether he has figured out how to make money online, he admitted that he hadn't and that the only comics creators which seem to have figured it out are those that offer collateral products (t-shirts, lunch boxes, action figures, etc.). It's the sale of these products that generate the cash for the online presence. If you were a cartoonist, how would you define your business? How would you create a sustainable business model?

- **Transportation:** Transportation provides another interesting example: if you trace the evolution of transportation in the US and the companies who were dominant in the various stages of mass and personal transportation starting with stage coach companies, to railroads, to automobiles, to aircraft manufactures and airlines, to high speed rail, it's virtually impossible to find an example of any company that defined its business in such a way that they moved from even one stage to another along the evolutionary curve. No stagecoach company got into the railroad business; no railroad or stagecoach company got into automobiles; none of these companies got into air travel, etc. Would you not expect airlines to dabble in high-speed rail? One can only imagine that this is due primarily to two factors: a lack of technological expertise (which can be bought) or a bad definition of what business they're in.

- **Healthcare:** When working with healthcare clients, I challenge them to define their business and, very often, they begin by describing their service lines (oncology, cardiology, orthopedics, etc.) and quickly work in the physical plant ('…a building or campus') and their geographic locations. The problem with this is that, according to some estimates, as much as 90% of healthcare can be 'delivered remotely using technology.

I chaired a conference in the mid-90s on the topic of the Internet and healthcare and Shaun Jones, MD, then a member of the Department of Defense's DARPA, got the attention of the room, mostly folks from large healthcare systems, when he said to illustrate a point: "Imagine, Mayo quality care, anywhere in the world". Some of the attendees heard 'quality care, anywhere in the world' but not the fact that the delivery was being done by the Mayo Clinic…and not by *their* organization. Given the cost and price pressures on the healthcare industry, I believe that massive transformation if the delivery of healthcare is about to change the healthcare industry in a way as profound as Amazon.com changed the book and online shopping industries.

Banks: Remember what banks were like a number of years ago: you had to physically visit a branch, make out a check to yourself to get cash (if it was later than 3pm on a Friday you were going to have to figure something else out until Monday morning), you would spend hours making out and mailing checks and balancing your checkbook every month. Today, most of the banking we do, including the ability to deposit a check via your cell phone's camera, is done remotely. The only time I ever visit my bank is when I need to access my safety deposit box or get a cashier's check.

- **Pharmacies:** Pharmacies are an interesting and emerging example. I obtained my last two flu shots from a pharmacy in NYC; it was an *impulse buy* given that I needed a flu shot and saw their sign. No appointment necessary, my insurance covered the shot and I was out of there in twenty minutes. I recently saw a Duane Reade drugstore in New York City with a sign that touted "Doctor on Duty in this Store". Tell me again what business pharmacies are in…and hospitals…and clinics. One of the corniest jokes I've heard in a while was that the bookstore chain, Borders, has considered placing physicians on their premises but decided against it. To advertise the fact that they were not going to put doctors in their stores, they were going to wage a marketing campaign called 'Borders Without Doctors'. Sorry.

Now, there's no guarantee that if you answer this question of what business you're in correctly that you'll be out of the woods. I'm sure that Polaroid defined theirs as *instant photography* for years…but I'm thinking as they mouthed those words, the mental image was of a chemically treated laminate of materials which, when exposed to light, captured photographic images and etched them onto a backing layer.

Fossil Fuels: Another example of where defining a business is tricky can be found in the oil and coal industries. I've heard of very expensive forays into one or the other of these businesses because they sound so similar to each other in terms of businesses: you locate the stuff and you take it out of the ground and sell it.

The problem is that there is a substantial difference in these similar-sounding businesses: for coal the easy part is finding it; the hard part is getting it out of the ground. The situation for oil is just the opposite: finding it is hard but, once you do, getting it out of the ground is fairly straightforward; simply shoot some buckshot into the ground to a depth and stand back...my source: The Beverly Hillbillies opening segment.

Defining The Business You're In Worksheet

In Defining The Business You're In, What Lessons Can You Learn From These Businesses In Terms Of Defining The Business That Your Organization Is In?

Organization	Similarities In Defining Your Business	Dissimilarities In Defining Your Business	Lessons
Buggy Whips			
Unites States Postal Services			
Media: TV, Movies, Music, Print			
Transportation			
Healthcare			
Banking			
Pharmacies			
Fossil Fuels			

Step 2 – Creating A Vision For Your Organization

Purpose: To create and commit to a Vision of what you want the organization to be within the 5 to 10 year horizon. This vision will inform and guide the rest of the process and it's critical that you get it right. The information/knowledge gained from defining the business that your organization is in will be extremely helpful in creating the Vision for your organization.

Outcome: The outcome of this step will be a graphic/visual representation of the Vision showing the various components, how they relate to each other and how, collectively they result in the desired end state for the organization.

You only have to skip this step once, under the mistaken belief that everyone knows and agrees upon what the vision for the organization is, to realize the power of this step. This is an opportunity to scope and define the organization before the group invests too much time arguing about the details without having a sense of what the 'whole' will look like. The following are some examples of the types of graphics you might generate during this exercise. Please note, you should not try to influence which of these representations the participants choose; we want this to be *their work* and to represent *their* vision of the future.

> *A Hierarchical Structure*: show the various components of a Vision and how they relate to each other hierarchically. Often these are represented by drawings of structures (houses, corporate offices, hospitals, etc.) with each level building upon the level beneath it and deriving its purpose from the level above.

The Value of the Hierarchical Structure representation: these are usually a fairly comprehensive view of what the vision is and what will be required to achieve the vision and how the various components will need to relate to each other.

Flow Diagram: a process flow as seen from a certain perspective, usually the customer showing the order in which events occur and how each event depend upon and feed other events.

The Value of Flow Diagrams: flow diagrams tend to give life to the vision by portraying a temporal (time-based) view and by showing, at a macro level, what is required to provide the envisioned experience.

Living Organism: often shown as plants or trees, this representation is similar to both the Hierarchical Structure and Flow Diagram with a little less rigor attached to dependencies and timing.

The Value of Living Organism Diagrams: Although, in my opinion, not as specific and, therefore, not as valuable as hierarchical or flow diagrams, the living organism often does an excellent job of expressing the passion and contributions of specific individuals in an organization and allows folks who think organically to both provide valuable input *and* to express the future in terms that are comfortable for them.

Other Representations:

- o *Concentric Circles – similar to hierarchies*
- o *Transportation (Car, plane, train) – similar to hierarchies*
- o *Customer Experience – similar to flow*

Step By Step Guide For Creating A Vision

I believe that this step is so critical to the success of an organization and the viability of their Strategic Plan that we're going to go into considerable detail to show you how to craft a Vision. There is an expanded version of this material in my book, *No More Meetings From Hell.*

Let's be clear before going any further with this technique. The outcome of this step, at least initially, *is not to create a vision statement.* It is to create a graphical representation of the shared *Vision* for the future (of the organization, the product, the solution, etc.). The difference between a carefully *wordsmithed* vision statement versus a detailed graphic representing the shared vision of the organization is similar to the difference in describing a new house in one, short paragraph vs. seeing an artist's rendering of the structure.

It's important that each participant have an opportunity to have their voices heard during the creation of the Vision. If there are too many individuals to allow each participant to construct their own individual vision, you can get excellent results by forming subgroups. The advantage to utilizing subgroups is that each member of the subgroup will have a greater opportunity to have their input heard than they would if meeting in the large group. If you choose the 'breakout group' route, be sure to give thought to pre-selecting the groups with the goal of as much diversity (status, years in the organization, group/department, style, power, etc.) as feasible.

Whether you choose individual or group vision graphics, the challenge will be to direct the creation of the vision graphic and then to synthesize the various visions into one.

Let's begin by reviewing the instructions that you'll give to the participants. Be clear that they are to draw a graphic of their vision and that the use of text is reserved only for labelling their diagrams. Expect pushback; you're asking them to work outside their comfort zone and not a lot of people welcome that. Have faith in the process and you'll be fine. Give them what I call a *starter kit* of what should be included in there Vision. Such things as:

- What Business the organization will be in;

- How the organization will be positioned in the market:

    o Luxury

    o High function

    o Inexpensive

    o Convenient

- o Etc.

- What products/services will be offered;

- What technologies will be used and how;

- The relationship between the organization and:

  - o Competitors

  - o Customers

  - o Suppliers

  - o Employees

  - o Etc.

- What geographies will be covered;

- What channels will be used to get the products/services to the market;

You're probably wondering how you can possibly synthesize the work of a large number of people into one graphic. If this seems daunting to you, imagine trying to build a strategic plan if there isn't a synthesized, agreed-upon and committed-to vision of what the group is trying to achieve. You can't get there from here!

I use this approach in almost every engagement I do and it always feels like 'working without a net'. I liken it to a jazz routine in that I know the overall theme but am never sure of the exact notes until I (and the group) actually play them.

Deciding On Individual vs. Small Group Work

As a general rule, if I have more than eight people in a group, I'll break them up into subgroups to create the vision graphic. Regardless of the approach you choose, you'll end up with multiple vision graphics needing to be synthesized. Below, when I refer to 'worst case scenario', there's part of me that is thrilled when the group is not in agreement! Why? Because we found this out before spending our precious time and energies on creating a solution only to find out that the wheels fall off because it didn't fit the vision of one or more members of the group. I'd rather know this as early as possible rather than spinning our wheels needlessly.

Worst case: Members of a subgroup can't agree

If you find that you have opposing ideas in a subgroup, have each 'position' prepare a vision graphic. When it's time to report out, explain that there is a disagreement (or two or three) and that we want to examine each of the models with the intent of coming to a consensus at some point down the road.

Reporting Out Of Breakout Groups

Give instructions to the whole group that their job is to listen to the report outs with two things in mind: what are the salient features of the vision that strike a chord in terms of being an important or defining feature that they want to see embodied in the synthesized vision and, as important, what does each vision either have in common with or in conflict with each other vision graphics.

You may be wondering what happens when members of each subgroup agree, but there is not agreement between subgroups.

This divergence of opinions will come to the larger groups' attention during the subgroup's report outs. You, on the other hand, will have gotten a head's up. How? During the small group work, you'll walk from group to group, help them get started if necessary and assess what they're creating. You'll begin to get a sense as to whether consensus is near or whether additional work needs to be done to reach consensus.

My experience has been that in almost every case, the groups will be close to consensus (at the macro-level) than anyone would've imagined. I've found that with the group's help and agreement, we can usually cut and paste various components from the vision graphs and combine the 'salient features' into one vision graphic which can then be used as a guide or the balance of the project.

Some concerns I can set to rest:

1. *Will everyone participate in what they might perceive as an unconventional approach?* Yes. Assuming you've created a spirit of trust and a sense that you're competent, even the highest ranking, crankiest, least playful member of the group will do this. My favorite example is when, during the first few minutes of the individual work of creating a graphic, the 'alpha male in the group mumbled to me as I walked by him "I'm not liking you very much right now", to which I replied "Just suck it up and do your damn work". He laughed and, at the end of the exercise, proclaimed to the rest of the group "We've never had this conversation before…this is amazing…and all Jack did was to give us drawing materials!"

2. *Will you get vision statements instead of graphics?* No. Not if you set the groundrules up front to only use text to label elements of the graphic and not for sentences.

3. *What happens if you can't reach consensus?* Bring in the champion and let him decide. Give each 'side' of the question ample time to present their thinking and resulting proposals and for the champion to ask questions. As long as everyone is heard and, even if half the group was seeing the vision as a different outcome, having the champion weigh in this early will allow the group to move forward. By the way, I've never had to resort to this step. Why? If the assumptions are level-set appropriately during the environmental scan, folks will be working from the same assumption set and will most likely come to the same or similar conclusions.

Step 3 – Identify Your Organization's Core Competencies

Note: In some organizations, doing this step *before* the creating the Vision may make more sense. In the majority of cases, however, identifying Core Competencies will be your second step. The question you'll need to answer is whether a robust Vision can be created without agreement about the organization's core competencies. The answer to that question will guide you as to the order in which to do the first two steps in the process.

The Incompetent Use Of Core Competence

The power or creating/recognizing and utilizing an organization's *core competence* is considerable when done properly. Get this right, and your Strategic Plan will be sustainable and will provide a barrier to entry for your competitors; get it wrong and the best you can hope for is a catchy marketing tag line and some really bitchin' t-shirts! Core competence first received wide focus due to an excellent article by Prahalad, and Hamel, in the 1990 article *The Core Competence of the Corporation*, in the Harvard Business Review (v. 68, no. 3) pp. 79–91. In their work, they give examples of well-known organizations and their core competencies such as Honda and the design and manufacture of engines, Sony and their Jedi Knight-like skills with miniaturization, Philips and their optical-media expertise, and Black and Decker's small electrical engine capabilities.

Typically, when I ask clients, even those who are familiar with the concept of core competence, what *their* organization's core competence is, I get one or more of the following responses:

- Dead silence;

- Wild guesses suggesting that they know the term core competence, but they themselves have no idea how to apply the concept;

- A specific, almost too quick, response which suggest that they've been asked the question before and thought about it.

In order to illustrate the problem that arises when core competence is misunderstood and misapplied, I'll share a story of a client that I worked with a few years ago.
The client's business was in the computer aftermarket. They were a division of a large high tech company and their mission was to provide add-on equipment to customers of the parent organization. I began my gig with this client by meeting with the senior management team and, as I often do when starting with a new client, I asked what they saw as their core competence.
The response was given quickly and everyone in the room nodded their heads in agreement; their core competence was *gathering, organizing and mining customer data.* They went on to say that, by virtue of a very large, sophisticated data base and state of the art software, they knew their clients inside and out and they used that knowledge to gain a competitive advantage over other suppliers (for those components that weren't proprietary and which were readily available from a number of sources). I thought to myself that if they really had this capability and knew how to leverage it, the barrier to entry for their competitors was significant. Nice!

We adjourned the meeting and I then spent some time with the front-line sales and support people. These are the folks who handled inbound and outbound calling with customers and attempted to optimize each call in terms of sales revenue and margin. They sat in a large area, separated by cubicles, and using headsets and computers, they spent the day working with customers....the very same customers I'd been told about by senior management, and knowledge about whom they stated as their core competence by virtue of their intergalactic computer system and data base.

After a few minutes of the sales representative telling me about her job, I asked her to demonstrate the customer information system which she used to pitch customers about products based on in-depth knowledge of those customers ...you know...their core competence. The rep grinned and opened her desk drawer that contained customer files; not computer files, but hard copy, last century's technology breakthrough, *hanging* file folders.

Convinced that she had misunderstood my question, I asked about the computer system again and this time the grin turned to a grimace as she began telling me how *nobody* uses that system because the data base is corrupt: duplicate entries, missing information, *incorrect information*, etc. She said that all of her colleagues had their own collection of customer information filed in these hanging folders and that's what they *all* used to support them during the sales process.

Well, this is what I get paid for: delivering really bad news in as direct a way as possible. You can imagine the reactions of the senior managers when I broke the news to them, but what surprised me more than anything was how they parsed the bad news as simply a small matter which could be fixed…no worries, mate…just a slight course correction. Management's reaction reminded me of Bob Newhart's routine about a submarine captain announcing to the crew that, in a few minutes they'd be once again gazing at the familiar skyline of Los Angeles….or New York City…in a tone that suggested it was no big deal that he wasn't sure where they were within 3,000 miles!

Here's what I imagined happened. At a Strategic Planning Retreat, the *idea* of the intergalactic database was introduced and through the clever use of *Projector Ware* techniques (a sarcastic term for software that only exists on PowerPoint slides), money was spent, systems were built and reports were made which totally mis-led management about the customer information system. Once management drank their own Kool Aid, they were off to the races and began piling on strategic initiatives dependent upon the system that never really worked in the first place. This is what management consultants live for.

This type of organizational denial is not unique to the private sector. In the early 1970s book, **The Greening of America** by Charles Reich spoke about military-industrial complex and the author was scheduled to speak at the Public Library in New Haven, CT. The author was not able to make the book reading due to weather problems, and the moderator, faced with an empty podium, asked folks who had read the book and had stories to tell, to join him on stage.

One of the folks who spoke had been in Vietnam and told the audience about a computer system that the Pentagon had spent millions on which was designed to pinpoint enemy positions for the commanders in the field. The unveiling of the finished computer system took place in front of Pentagon brass and members of Congress *in Vietnam*. The only problem was, the system was a failure and never worked. The brass decided that, rather than fess up to this monumental failure, they would bogey up the data to appear as if the system was working.

In a clearing, in Vietnam, the system was demoed to the approving comments of all those assembled. The system showed that the closest enemy position was a few miles away. When the demo was completed, the lights were turned on and, much to the dismay of the assembled crowd, they found themselves within sight of enemy troops!

Organizations tend to thrive on this kind of deceit and do little to discourage it. If you want your organization to thrive, you might want to start with your culture and begin rewarding honesty.

In any event, more often that not, the response to the question 'What is your organization's core competence' is met with a response which easily fits into the *mom and apple pie* rubric; for example:

- We're customer centered;

- We have caring people;

- We provide the best quality for the money;

- Our brand name;

- Many locations:

- Best locations;

- Etc.

The problem with these answers is that:

- They're most-likely not true;

- They cannot be proved;

- They're easily duplicated by well-financed and aggressive competitors if the payoff to them is large enough.

Doing Core Competence Well

In my experience, the most difficult part of this step is getting to a level of honesty and self-assessment that many organizations simply do not possess. Most cultures discourage this behavior and, instead, reward managers for supporting each other in meetings, covering up or not discussing short-comings in current operations and future plans. The *deal* is 'I won't ask the hard questions of you if you agree to support my programs and not ask hard questions of me'. This makes for comfortable staff meetings and really bad strategies. It also masks the truth from senior management and allows them to make erroneous assumptions, and make disastrous *bets* on the future of the organization.

The places where total honesty about your core competencies is absolutely critical to the future of your organization:

- Market Share and trend: what is the organization's market share and is it shrinking, stagnant or growing; as hard as it may be to accept, there are people who do not want the market share known for fear of reprisal. This is especially true if the share is shrinking or stagnant;

- Competition: who are your competitors and what are their core competencies. How do your products & services match up in terms of critical elements such as price, quality, service, customer satisfaction, etc. In many organizations the culture supports and rewards a macho perspective that criticizes and minimizes competition and overstates the value of their own products, services and organization. Deadly.

- Understanding and use of critical technologies: woe to the organization that thinks that technology won't affect their industry. Does your organization *get that*? Clearly the Internet is a major part of the competitive landscape. What is frightening is watching an organization which is behind its competitors put up their first website; often it is little more than an online brochure, and generally doesn't add any real functionality that would attract (or retain) customers and potential customers. My experience is that the bulk of visitors to this type of site and initial foray onto the Internet are managers showing it off to themselves, family members and friends.

- One of the more interesting examples of the use of an online presence is QVC in that they have been a very successful retailer on TV for years which depended on a relationship established between their on-air hosts and the home viewer. When they began to see their market share eroding, they went to work to find ways create an online presence without the benefits of the relational nature of their TV presence. Since so much of their TV presence is the *talk show* and chatty feel to their sales pitches, this was no easy task. In a recent interview with the NY Times Mike George, QVC's Chief Executive says that "...first-time buyers on QVC.com might not be loyal to QVC, but that e-mail marketing could help convert them. We know that if you don't make a repeat purchase in 90 days, you're probably not going to," he says. "We're able to decipher, based on what product you came in on, what other items might be of interest to you." He also says that message boards, ratings and other social features on QVC.com do promote a sense of community and that "their usage level is very high." (*Source NY Times, November 20, 2010 "Can QVC Translate Its Pitch Online?"*)

- Your People: how motivated and educated are your people? How do you know? How do customers feel about your people? How do your people feel about each other and their managers? Don't kid yourself into thinking that the answer to these questions is positive. Just spend a few days observing the people you interact with as a customer of *another* organization. Do you honestly think that *their* management is aware of how badly they treat customers? Really?

Getting Your Core Competence As Right As You Can; Start With Your Salespeople and Customers

Let me be clear: the correct answer to the question 'What is your organization's core competence and/or competitive advantage'…might just be 'we don't have one'. There is nothing to say that the reason you've been successful and are still in business might be due simply to being in the right place at the right time or having a lead in the market which, although historically important, isn't defensible and you're about to get rolled by new entrants (competitors).

As sad as that prospect is, it would be even sadder if your organization had a core competence and failed to recognize and leverage it. I believe that the organization that can identify and leverage its core competence can stomp its competitors simply by becoming more focused in its use of their core competence.

So, how do you go about finding out what you're really good at? The problem is that the people who are furthest from the answer are probably not the folks you meet with on a regular basis; you know, the senior management team.

In my experience, senior managers too often have created a wide chasm between themselves and the folks who can answer the questions that need answering in order to put together a strategic plan. If you were to get these folks to tell you the truth, they'd probably say that one of the best things about being a senior manager in the organization is that they rarely, if ever, have to listen to customers and sales people talk about what's not right with the organization's products, services and organization. Why? Well, for one thing, no one likes to hear criticisms.

Even Steve Jobs, who I consider to be a consummate strategist, when told that holding the new iPhone 4 in a certain way all but killed it's cell signal is reported to have responded 'well, don't hold it that way'. He was probably fed up with hearing complaints about the product but, I gotta' tell ya', he's not alone in his attitude when it comes to receiving feedback from the market.

Look, you want direct feedback about what your organization is good at what it sucks at? Get out of your office for two weeks and visit your best salespeople and then, with them, visit some of your best and worst customers…ask them the question…and then shut the hell up while they answer you. By the way, the choice of these customers is critical. Find the most representative, most-loyal, crankiest and least comfortable ones to visit. Don't leave it up to your salespeople solely to pick the customers; they'll pick the ones that will say the things *they* want you to hear and they'll pick the ones with whom they have the best relationship.

Your first instinct will be to debate them. Don't. You'll just piss them off and shut them down. Just listen, take lots of notes and only offer a counter argument if they've gotten something wrong...something like...'you know, we haven't done a good job of explaining it, but our Model W23x unit won't explode in your face if you simply hit the function key *before* hitting the turbo key; I appreciate this feedback and we're going to work on fixing this or least do a better job of explaining it in the future.

What I am *not* talking about here is a sterile, often inaccurate *survey* of your customers but a good, old-fashioned, sit-down. Get face-to-face, raw feedback unfiltered by anyone. It's getting to the point where I can't use a public restroom without receiving a request to fill out a survey about my experience. What started off as an effort to gather customer opinions and experiences has turned into a major annoyance!

What can you expect to hear from your salespeople and customers? I'll use product feedback as an example in the following list, but you can substitute *services* just as easily:

- What your product/service does well and what it needs to have in order to be really good;

- What it would take for them to buy more of it; if they don't offer this, you can ask it at the end of the conversation. You can expect price to be on the list, but my guess is that they'd buy more at the same or higher price if your product met their needs better than it does today;

- What about your product is terrible and what your competitors' products do better;

- What your competitors are talking about in the next
release of *their* product. No! Don't ask that question
directly but, rather, ask them where they think the
market is going over the next couple of years.

The other key to getting good feedback is to choose the right
salespeople: not only the ones that suck up to you every time
they see you); get a few *royal pains in the ass* in the mix as
well…you know, the ones you typically avoid at sales
meetings because they never seem to stop complaining and
they always make you feel uncomfortable and challenged. If
they have crappy ideas or they are ill informed, take them off
the list…but make sure that you're reacting to that and not
that you can't stand to talk to them. By the way, the noisy
salespeople are often the opinion-leaders in the field
organization. Get them involved in improving your products
and you've developed an in-house marketing arm that money
can't buy!

I will expand on how to use core competencies in *Creating The
Design Center of Strategies* below.

Core Competence Worksheet

What is your organization exemplary at? Be specific and ask yourself, 'how do I know and can I prove it?'

When is the last time someone took the time to speak with your best salespeople and customers to find out the *real* reason people buy (or not) your product or service and what it would take for them to buy more.

Step 4. Creating The *Design Center* Of Strategies

This step is the most difficult and, for that reason and a few others, it is generally what I find as the most glaring omission to most strategic plans. This step defines the strategic *driver* for your plan. It is the *Design Center* that will provide the primary competitive advantage for the organization. Why, then, doesn't every company have a compelling strategic plan built around a Design Center? Let me be clear, the term *Design Center* is simply a way to refer to the strategic driver…call it whatever you like. There's no magic in the term. The main reason is that it requires an amazing amount of honesty about the organization and, in many cases, an investment in making the design center an actionable reality.

I've borrowed the term *Design Center* from the computer industry; it refers to the core ideas upon which a computer architecture is built. In creating a set of strategies, one of the most critical steps is to decide what you'll use as the key drivers of those strategies.

Some examples of some common *Design Centers*:

• Ubiquitous Locations: physical/virtual presence in more places than any competitor. Key to leveraging this driver is that the locations match up with the demographics of your current and potential customers. Having stores in dying shopping malls doesn't count. Once you've chosen this as the design center of your strategy, how are you going to leverage your locations to your strategic advantage?

- o Previously mentioned Duane Reade is seemingly on every corner of every street in New York City. Clearly their strategy involves being ubiquitous and it will be interesting to see how they leverage this strategy in the future;

- o Starbucks strategy of, seemingly, putting a Starbucks in every empty storefront in the world backfired on them a few years ago when they found themselves over-extended financially. I heard a comic remark that Starbucks had just opened a Starbucks inside the men's room of his Starbucks. In addition, many corporate cafeterias, bookstores and hospital restaurants as well as supermarkets sell Starbucks' brand products. The question here becomes one of cannibalization (no, not that kind of cannibalization!!) of one store by other stores and other outlets. When identical stores are as close to each other as Starbucks stores have become, especially in major cities, the risk becomes one of taking business from each other. Starbucks is a perfect example of the risks and payoffs that come from a strategy build on being *everywhere.*

- Complete/comprehensive product/service line: this refers to the concept of *one stop shopping* and the convenience factor that draws customers in. Customers will often endure other shortcomings just to be able to get everything that they need in one place. I live on a sailboat and, as you can imagine, I buy a lot of *sailboat stuff.* Our local marine supply store is notorious for high prices, unknowledgeable salespeople and the most dishonest and arrogant owner imaginable! Why shop there, you ask? Simple, they have a better selection of everything than any place within 30 miles. If you stand in their parking lot you can observe customers taking a deep breath as the brace themselves for what they know is going to be a terrible experience.

Walmart: The ability to drive to one location, park in one lot and gather up groceries, clothing, medications, eye glasses, housewares, etc. at a reasonable price is a pretty hefty barrier to entry.

- Creator of Technology Solutions:

  Intel: How'd you like to be in an industry where the pace of change looks like what's known as Moore's Law: *The number of transistors that can be placed on an integrated circuit doubles every two years.* I'm sorry, did you say the capacity *doubles every two years*! I did!!! The law is named after Gordon Moore, one of the founders of Intel, but that doesn't mean he owns the playing field; he's just credited with describing the pressure of operating in the market. You see, this law impacts everything we value about electronics, especially computers: size, weight, speed and features. For a while, Intel was being threatened by AMD, their major competitor. The strategy that Intel chose was to focus on their core products, processors and chipsets with a vengeance.

- First To Market With New Features/Technologies: American Airlines: The archetype for this strategy is the reservations system that American Airlines introduced in *the early 60s* called the Semi-Automated Business Research Environment (Sabre). In 1976

American made the system available to travel agents. Armed with this tool, travel agents could make reservations with their client seated in front of them or while they were on the phone, in a matter of minutes. Although other airlines' flights were listed on the system, being *first to market* enabled American to tilt the playing field so much in their direction that their competitors had to take them to court. You see, it turns out if you're a busy travel agent, it isn't going to be in your interest to pour through pages and pages of flights looking for a deal. Instead, in the majority of cases, the travel agent would choose the flight on the first line of the screen…which, because it was American's system…was *always* an American Airlines flight. The advantage of being first in a market can be huge. This isn't always a slam-dunk as the previously cited Barnes & Noble example of the e-reader shows.

Apple's first iPhone had lots of shortcomings, but the capability was so far beyond anything in the market at the time, that buyers jumped on it with both feet in spite of bugs, being limited to AT&T, too few apps, etc. The driver was that Apple was the first company to produce a phone anything like it!

- <u>Heavily Discounting/Giving Away One Or More Of Your Products/Services</u>

  Printers: This technique most likely started in the grocery business where deals on certain items that yielded littler or no margin were used to draw customers into the store. Once there, they weren't about to buy only the sale item(s); they'd do all of their grocery shopping for the week. Google, razor blades, printers and print cartridges are examples of this strategy. I realized the printer example first hand when I found that I could buy a new printer (which came with three cartridges) cheaper than I could buy the three replacement cartridges alone!

  Since then, the printer companies have wised up and they offer *sample-sized* cartridges with their printers. This requires that, within a month or so, you'll be purchasing their cartridges at full price.

- <u>Build Unassailable Customer Loyalty</u>

  Southwest Airlines: Combine over-the-top customer service, employees who are passionate about what they do and supportive tactics such as not charging for baggage while every other airline was doing it, and you have a business that has built, legitimately, world class customer loyalty.

  Apple: This is a photo of a line outside of one Apple's European stores on the day they released the iPhone 4.

There's nothing I can add to this scene other than to say that this photo is a de facto definition of *customer loyalty*. It transcends common sense, it keeps the customer at the table (or in a tent on the sidewalk) and it's damn hard to accomplish or defeat.

If you want a sense as to how to build this type of customer loyalty, take a look at Apple's products. Pay attention to how well thought-out and designed they are and how, through software updates (e.g. the iPhone IOS 4 software), Apple keeps adding value to their phones, computers and iPods without charging the customer exorbitant fees in the process. Customers who owned the iPhone 3G and 3Gs received free updates to bring them to IOS 4.0.

What was brilliant about this was that the new hardware, the new iPhone itself, had remarkably new and powerful features and once you saw the *some of those same features (but not all)* on the older phones, it made you yearn of the new hardware features as well. Don't be deluded into thinking that this is the whole story. Apple creates really innovative products, they redefine almost every market they're in and Steve Jobs is a master and communicating what he wants people to believe.

- <u>Rapid Adoption of Emerging Technologies</u>:

  This *design* center can either be based on your organization creating new technologies or, more likely, adopting them as soon as they've been proven. Mercedes Benz and BMW are both examples of companies who adopt emerging technologies ahead of the rest of the market. The risk to your organization in adopting this strategy is that you might come into the market with new technologies too early, before they are tested in the market, and bet a fortune on the *wrong horse*. You'll also open the door to the next entrant.

  There are real advantages to being the second entrant in that you can learn from the mistakes (or successes) of the first entrant. The question for your organization is whether you have a core competence in assessing, choosing and implementing technologies that you can trust to make the right decisions re: early adoption. Another key question is how much of a head start can you get on the rest of the market by adopting emerging technologies early?

- <u>Your People</u>: This one is tricky. You hardly ever hear managers say 'our people really suck, they don't do well with customers, they don't really care and they don't know our products very well'. Think of how many times you, as a customer, have had that reaction to people you've dealt with in other organizations.

  It's more likely that you'll hear some pabulum about *'our people are our most important asset'*. Interestingly, one of the organizations that I (and others) have experienced as first-rate in terms of their people and their interactions with customers is the IRS…yes *the Internal Revenue Service.*

- Low Cost: Hyundai's strategy is to offer more value than their competitors at a lower price. I remember the first time I saw the ***Friends Don't Let Friends Drive Hyundais*** bumper sticker; it summed up everything we knew about this cheap South Korean import at the time.

  Hyundai has come a long, long way from their 1986 debut in the U.S. with the very sketchy Excel. Starting in 2001 with the *Santa Fe*, a small SUV that helped define that market, they have steadily gained market share and developed a loyal following for their fleet of vehicles. They were the first automaker to offer a 10-year, 100,000-mile warranty and that was enabled by a heavy commitment to and investment in quality. That put them on the consumer's radar screen.

  Then, during the freefalling economy in 2009, Hyundai advertised that their customers could return their cars if their lost their job. Think about how bold both of these moves were in terms of financial risk…but then again, if you are *walking the walk* of quality you can offer that kind of warranty without much risk *and* speaking of walking, even folks who lose their jobs need transportation. At last count, about 100 cars were returned…but the PR boost Hyundai received was enormous. They blitzed the Super Bowl with their commercials and timed it just as Toyota was against the ropes with a number of highly publicized quality issues.

Southwest Airlines is an example of low cost. Wait, Southwest Airlines has incredible customer loyalty, some of the best people in the any industry *and low prices*....they must be bleeding red ink, right?

Well, no. As a matter of fact, they are the largest airline of any in terms of passengers and have made a profit for the past 37 years. Last year, it flew 86 million passengers, more than any other airline within the United States. It operates 3,200 flights a day, owns a fleet of 544 planes and serves 69 domestic cities from Seattle to Fort Lauderdale, Fla., and from Lubbock, Tex., to Buffalo (Source: NY Times November 21, 2010). On the other hand, if you want to see how to really *piss off* your employees and your customers, hop aboard almost any other domestic airline where the prices are high, the service is terrible (the people who interact with customers are rude and angry and the spaces between seats barely allows for the wearing of eyeglasses, never mind opening a laptop) and the total experience makes driving look good in comparison.

McDonald's is an example of a company that has built an empire based on low cost and ubiquitous locations. You walk into any McDonald's anywhere in the world and you know that you can get a low cost meal and a crash dummy test for your Lipitor.

• Offensive & Defensive Strategies

Many companies, once they've built the *mental muscle* to do so, become adept at creating *offensive* strategies like the ones listed above. The really good companies are also quite skilled at crafting *defensive* strategies as well.

Some examples of defensive strategies:

o Where location is important, buying up desirable properties/businesses to block competition from coming in; you'll often see this approach used in healthcare and fast food;

o It's not unheard for companies to run ads looking for certain skills in certain geographies/businesses not with the intent of hiring or locating there, but as a *head fake* to the competition;

o Buying up all/some the resources (people, raw materials, production equipment, etc.) to keep competition out of the game;

o One excellent example of a defensive strategy was AT&T's exclusive agreement with Apple to sell iPhones. Most consumers would never pick AT&T based on other factors (their network *had* a terrible reputation at the time) but switched their service to them in order to gain access to the iPhone. Early in 2011 the availability of iPhones on other networks, especially Verizon, is most likely going to happen, but AT&T was able to gain a significant foothold while they had the exclusive arrangement with Apple.

One of the critical distinctions you'll need make is the difference between your strategies for entering a market vs. your steady-state strategy. The example of the introduction of word processing software through legal departments is a good example of an entry strategy which, once the capabilities of word processing became known and desired, is different than a strategy for gaining and keeping dominance in the market.

Creating The Design Center Worksheet

What can you learn from these companies in creating the *Design Center* for your strategies?

Key Strategic Design Center	Examples	Lessons	Lessons Applied To Your Organization
Ubiquitous Locations	Walmart Starbucks		
Comprehensive Product/Service Lines	Walmart		
Creator of Technology Solutions	Intel		
First To Market With New Features/Technologies	American Airlines (Historically)		
Give Away/Discount Product In Order To Sell Replacements	Printers/ Razors		
Build Unassailable Company Loyalty	Apple Southwest Airlines		
Rapid Adoption Of Emerging Technology	Mercedes Benz BMW		
People	Southwest Airlines		

…continued on next page

..continued from previous page

Low Cost	Southwest Airlines McDonald's		
Defensive/Lock-out Strategy	AT&T		

Step 5. Create The Dynamics Of Your Strategic Plan

Too often, Strategic Plans consist of flat lists of goals and/or objectives, unrelated collections of parts without any integration or tying together of those parts to and suffer from a lack of a systemic whole. One of my favorite examples of how strategies need to be dynamic and integrated is Google.

In the diagram below, which I created based on what I *inferred* from what I know about Google and its strategies, notice how the activities in State 1 are designed to create the environment and dynamics to enable Stages 2 and 3 to be successful.

When the Wall Street Journal got it wrong about Google and its ability to generate a profit they were focusing only on what they could see at the time...the *free* stuff shown in the first box in Stage 1 below. In fact, if Google's total strategy had been simply in that bounded part of the diagram below, the WSJ would've been correct and Google eventually would've gone out of business or become a niche player with support from crowdsourcing or the open source movement.

The *Inferred* Strategy
Notice The Dynamic Nature Of It

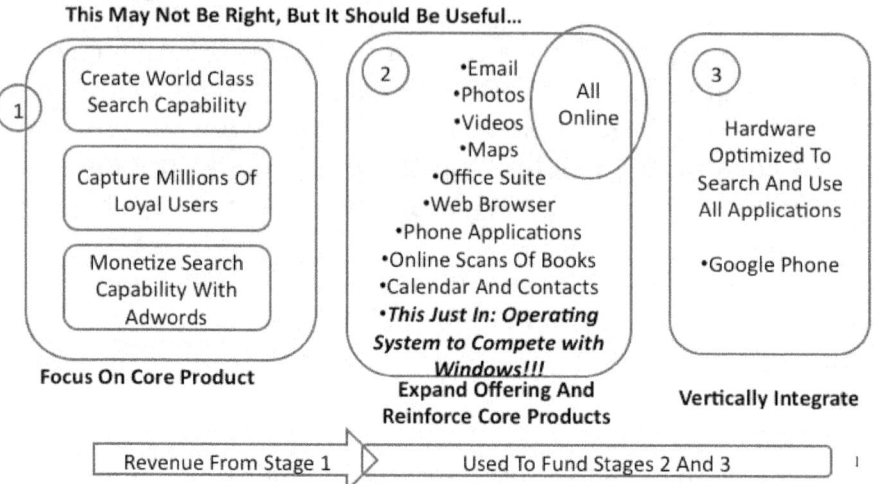

Google

This May Not Be Right, But It Should Be Useful...

1
Create World Class Search Capability

Capture Millions Of Loyal Users

Monetize Search Capability With Adwords

Focus On Core Product

2
•Email
•Photos
•Videos
All Online
•Maps
•Office Suite
•Web Browser
•Phone Applications
•Online Scans Of Books
•Calendar And Contacts
•*This Just In: Operating System to Compete with Windows!!!*

Expand Offering And Reinforce Core Products

3
Hardware Optimized To Search And Use All Applications

•Google Phone

Vertically Integrate

Revenue From Stage 1 ▷ Used To Fund Stages 2 And 3

Copyright 2010 Jack Rahaim, All Rights Reserved

Please Note: I created this diagram and, although it might not be totally right, it should be useful! The purpose is to show that strategies and tactics should exist to support and amplify each other. Think of this diagram dynamically, reading from left to right and notice how Google built the early capabilities as a device to get them to the middle and later stages.

Getting Carried Away With Dynamics

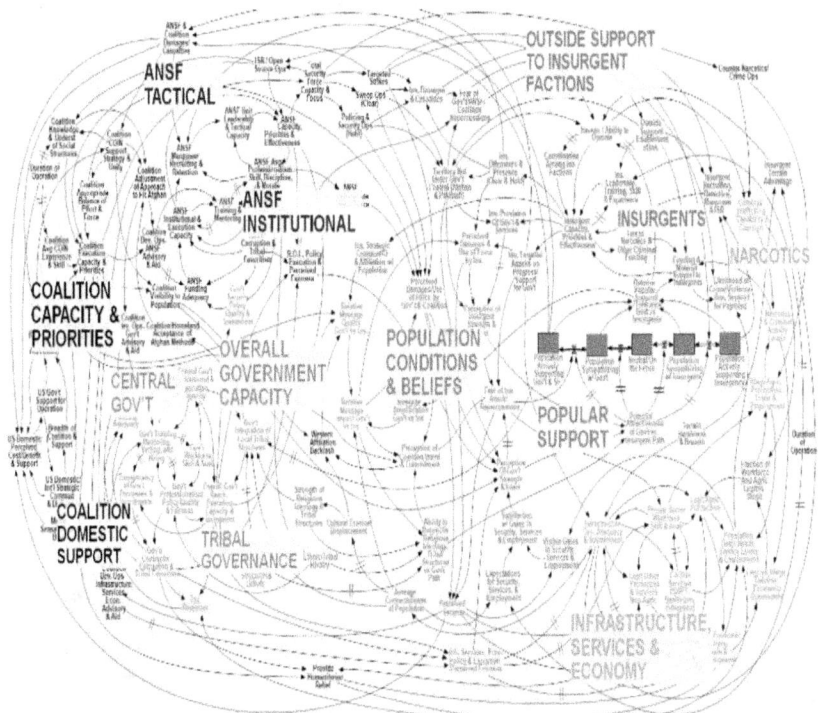

This is an actual strategy diagram from the US Government re: Afghanistan. I have nothing to add other than someone has certainly given this a lot of thought. The problem with a model of this many dynamics is that you have to hold certain factors constant in order to get this model to resolve...and the choice of those specific factors is the real strategy. The other problem with this diagram is that it is incomprehensible except to the people who drew it.

The following diagram illustrates how all parts of plan need to plug and play together and need to have a dynamic reason for being. It's not a Strategic Plan, but it shows system dynamics in action. This is a graphic of how Hewlett Packard envisioned a dynamic system where each part of the system has a reason unto itself *and* plays a role in the system as a whole. If you can apply a similar perspective to your strategies showing how each component fits into and supports the whole, you will be able to illustrate to yourself and others, the dynamics of your plan.

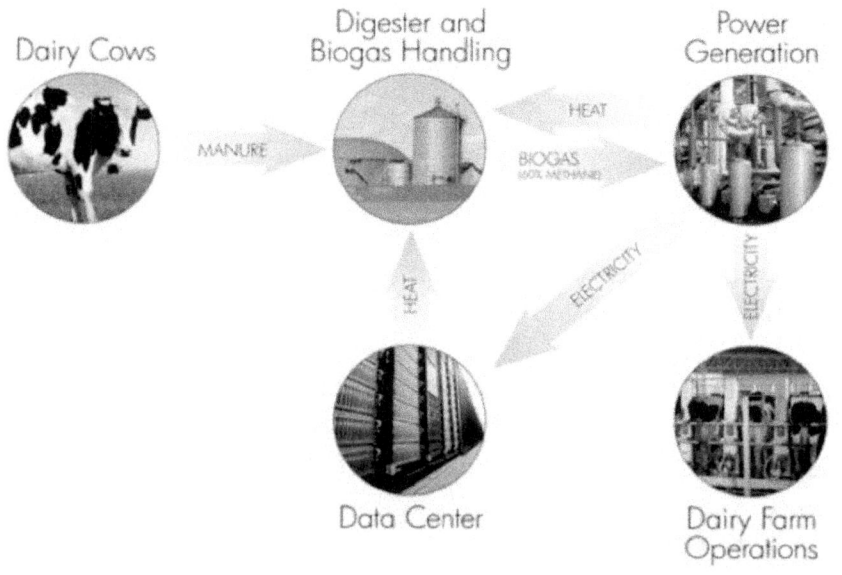

HP Labs Design for a Farm Waste
Data Center Ecosystem

Create The Dynamics Of Your Strategic Plan Worksheet

Think of this exercise as building one of those domino structures where each domino has two functions: one is to fall down and, equally important role each piece has is to knock down one or more dominoes in its path.

Sequence your strategies such that they reinforce and enable each other. Like dominoes, each strategy should exist for what it delivers in and of itself *and* for what it can deliver in terms of the other strategies. Look at the Google example again wherein they attracted *eyeballs* by offering world class free search services and then leveraged the audience that they build to be able to sell Adwords and other for fee services.

Stage 1 Strategies – and how they will enable later Stage (2, 3, ...n) Strategies:

Stage 2 Strategies – and how they're enabled by which Stage 1 Strategies and what they enable in Stage 3 and beyond.

Populate out to Stage 'n' where you've included all the Strategies and their relationship to the each other.

The Process of *Selling* The Strategic Plan

One of the common misconceptions on the part of planners is that once an organization has the *right* strategy, it's simply a matter of executing it. One of my favorite comments on this is that 'Culture eats strategy for lunch' meaning that regardless of how profound the Strategic Plan is for an organization, unless the organization understands it and commits to making it happen (and is rewarded for it by the culture of the organization) it simply is not going to happen.

Here's what works well:

- Create a compelling executive summary *and* presentation which provides the target audience a sense of the *journey* and the thinking that resulted in the plan; i.e., help them understand the thought process.

- If there is to be a presentation to the Board or your Executive Team, have someone with power and who is a major thought influencer give it; I can't tell you how many times I've seen elegant plans go up in smoke because of *how* they were presented and *who* did the presenting.

- Pre-sell the plan. I learned years ago that you never go into a meeting without knowing the outcome in advance; sit down with the key leaders in the group and walk them through the thinking and tease out any issues/*hot buttons* that should be addressed before the formal presentation. Too many times a plan gets diffused because of objections that could've been anticipated and dealt with prior to a critical meeting and a public smack down.

- Assign an influential, powerful senior manager or Board Member to be the Champion for the plan and consider assigning other managers/board members to champion pieces of the plan. You can count on resistance to change and you need to have the organizational *muscle* in place to move organizational barriers out of the way.

- Include a macro-level plan for implementation and reviews in the Strategic Plan. This isn't the detailed project plan…it's an overview of what will happen after the Strategic Plan is approved. Absent a plan to implement, you could've saved yourself and your colleagues a lot of time and sent them to a Broadway Show instead and gotten as much out of the process.

- Include a plan to authentically align departmental plans to the strategic plan; this takes a lot of time and work due to the tendency of managers to engage in *Agenda Bending* (more on this in a moment). Unless the managers understand the plan and unless senior managers understand what each department is planning, you lose the connection between intent and implementation.

- Build in measurement and feedback:

    o To assess whether the organization is on plan or not;

    o To measure the impact of the plan.

- o   To provide *early warning* of changes in the environment:

    - ▪   Competitors and their services, products, hiring patterns, etc.;

    - ▪   The economy;

    - ▪   Technology;

    - ▪   Etc.

- o   To continually remind the key leaders to what's been committed to both short and long term.

Expect And Plan For Resistance To The Change

Here is a short list of the reasons meaningful change often fails to be implemented in organizations due to resistance; feel free to add to this list based on your own experience:

- •   Too few people *really* believe in the plan:

    - o   Lack of understanding of what the plan proposes to do and why;

    - o   Lack of involvement/input in creating the plan;

    - o   The plan was conceived and written by people who are detached from the reality of the business who have latched onto the latest management fad;

- o People who don't have a comprehensive view of the market, the future of technology, etc., , competition, legislation, etc., cannot and will not get it.

- People believe in the plan, but are convinced that it will never be implemented. Why? Because there have been other *really good* plans which were introduced with great fanfare and which never saw the light of day.

- People are already stretched too thin just doing their day-to-day jobs and haven't got the time or energy to put into changing the organization;

- Historically, these kinds of changes weren't accompanied by resources to implement them;

- Sabotage: if there is a perceived shift in power from one department/individual to another you can expect there to be overt and covert sabotage.

- Despair: some organizations have been so pummeled by the environment and their competition that they just don't believe they have any chance to change their future…are they right? The answer to whether they're right or not is directly dependent upon the quality of the work you've done in creating the plan.

Overcoming Resistance To Change Worksheet

Given the above reasons that people resist organizational change, create a list of ways to prevent/deal with each type of resistance:

Implementation

I could write an entire series on books on how organizations screw up implementing strategic plans. Look, if you're not prepared to throw the organization's full power and resources behind implementing the plan that you've created, then you've just set your organization up for failure, burnt whatever good will you had with the managers who were involved in creating the plan and given your competition a pass to eat your lunch.

Guy Kawasaki, one of Apple's primary personalities and chief *evangelist*, says "What makes companies very successful and what makes companies fail is the same thing: it's a passionate adherence to a *strategy*".

I mentioned earlier the old chestnut that *'Culture eats Strategy for lunch'*. If you've watched your organization botch opportunities for success in the past, you should know what you need to do implement.

The topic of *implementation* is too broad to do justice to in a book primarily about strategy, but I will offer some critical pieces that you'll need to plan for:

Create A Detailed Plan

- What needs to be done?
- When?
- Who is responsible for the whole plan?
- Who is responsible for the pieces of the plan?
- What needs to precede and what needs to follow each step (dependencies)?

- How will changes to the plan be introduced, reviewed and decided; this is to avoid what is lovingly called *scope creep* where the project grows out of control (and out of budget) through incremental changes;
- Review cycles – i.e., when is the implementation going to be reviewed and by whom?
- Exit criteria: when will a project go from one stage (e.g. *design*) to the next stage (e.g. *build*) and who decides this?
- Doneness criteria: what will constitute *completed* segments and the total plan?

Utilize Project Management Techniques

- Assign a Project Manager who has a history of getting things done and support him or her with a senior manager Champion;
- Utilize the *appropriate* Project Management Tool; this may be a simple manual tool or a complex automated tool…let the size and complexity of the program determine which tool gets used.

Involve Senior Management

- As mentioned earlier, you can expect organizational resistance to change;
- Senior managers must see their role in making the implementation a success;
- What happens when a senior manager is the barrier? There needs to be a process to bring this attention to the person ultimately responsible for the success of the plan…and I always recommend that this be the CEO or Board Chair.

Have Frequent Reviews & Identify Problems Quickly

You'd be amazed how long some teams can go off target or struggle and the information doesn't reach anyone who can do anything about it for months; don't let this happen. Schedule frequent reviews (more frequent early, fewer as you gain momentum and confidence)

Pilot Ideas Early And Fail Forward

- Ideas always act differently when implemented;
- Pilot big ideas early and, if the idea is a failure, learn from the failure and 'fail forward';
- When you run the pilot, keep your hands off it until it runs its course. Tinkering with a pilot is not a fair approximation of how it would run in the real world.

Agenda Bending – The Art Of Managers Bending What They Are Already Doing To Look As If It's In Alignment With The Strategic Plan

Aligning departmental plans with the Strategic Plan is an exercise not unlike what the best catchers in major league baseball do: if a pitch isn't over the strike zone, they move their mitt as they catch it so that the pitch *appears* to have been over the plate. Let's see, they haven't changed the pitch, just the appearance of the pitch. All over the world, managers have developed significant skill in taking what they had already planned to do and *moving their mitts* by rewording their plans, tossing in the relevant *buzz phrases du jour*, and making them *appear* to align with the Strategic Plan.

This is not meant to be an indictment of what managers do in these situations; in many cases, they are making logical decisions based on what they *believe* is right for the organization. In some cases, they are creating plans that will justify their budgets and headcounts and, in order to do that, they have to *move their mitts* so that their plans look like they're in alignment with what the organization is professing through its strategic plan. My estimate is that 95% of you reading this book have done (or will do) the same thing at some point in your career.

The Strategic Planning process usually encourages this behavior by asking managers to fill out forms that place the organization's goals/strategies in columns and ask that the plans of the departments be shown in alignment with those goals/strategies.
Can you imagine how this exercise would've worked at Apple when it was only a computer manufacturer and someone in the organization was working on an iPod or iPhone concept?

The only way in which those products would have made sense is if they were part of a *strategy* to expand into those markets. The indictment here isn't of managers who engage in Agenda Bending, it's of the Strategic Planning process itself. This is the kind of behavior we can expect if the process for creating strategies is irrelevant, non-inclusive and focused on creating an artifact as opposed to creating strategic direction.

Sadly, most plans don't deserve the full attention of your line managers; they may have been fooled once into thinking that the planning process actually meant something, but when the plan is basically an exercise in formatting and data dumping and when budgets and staffing aren't aligned with the plan, managers quickly learn that the process is a charade and any work on it must be dispatched as quickly and as painlessly as possible.

Worksheet For Implementation

Inventory Of How Your Organization Sabotages Change

Ways In Which Your Organization Sabotages Change	Ways You Proactively Keep This From Happening

Richard Beckhard, a master educator in the area of change management talks about the skills and structures required to manage meaningful change. One of the key takeaways, in my opinion, is that the skills and structures required to be successful in any change effort *are different* based on what is to be managed:

- The current state and current business;

- The transition, i.e., the movement from where your organization is now to where it wants to be in the future;

- The future/desired state.

To restate this, you'll need to think through what it will take to keep the current state operational while managing the transition, and once you get to the future state. Beckhard argues, and I totally agree, that the skills and organizational structure for each of these is *different!*

Summary

I've tried to paint a balanced picture of how difficult it is to create strategies and how, with the right mind-set and tools, that it is possible for your organization to have a defensible position in your market for many years.

If you carry away any messages at all from this book, I'd like them to be:

1. Decide what business(es) the organization is in;

2. Determine your core competencies and engage your customers and your organization in defining them;

3. Have a compelling Mission and Vision towards which every individual is working;

4. Utilize every method you can to maximize and leverage your core competencies against competition and to utilize their weaknesses against them;

5. Learn from other organizations' success and failures;

6. Work hard at it…this is not easy, but it is doable.

Need help? I can be reached through my website:
www.emeetingmaker.com

www.ingramcontent.com/pod-product-compliance
Lightning Source LLC
Chambersburg PA
CBHW051541170526
45165CB00002B/823